THE
TRADITIONAL LATIN
MASS EXPLAINED

THE
TRADITIONAL LATIN
MASS EXPLAINED

DOM PROSPER GUÉRANGER

ABBOT OF SOLESMES

✠

Foreword by

Peter Kwasniewski

 Angelico Press

This Angelico edition is a supplemented
republication of the work originally published as
*Explanation of the Prayers and Ceremonies of Holy Mass:
Taken from Notes Made at the Conferences
of Dom Prosper Guéranger, Abbot of Solesmes.*

Translated from the French by
Rev. Dom Laurence Shepherd, O S B in 1885.

© Angelico Press 2017
Foreword © Peter Kwasniewski 2017

For information, address:
Angelico Press
169 Monitor Street
Brooklyn, NY 11222
angelicopress.com
info@angelicopress.com

978-1-62138-318-5 (pbk)
978-1-62138-319-2 (cloth)
978-1-62138-320-8 (ebook)

CONTENTS

FOREWORD

The liturgy is the highest and the holiest expression of the thought and intelligence of the Church, simply because it is carried out by the Church in direct communication with God, in confession, in prayer and praise.[1]

—Dom Prosper Guéranger

ROSPER LOUIS PASCAL GUÉRANGER (1805–75) was ordained a priest in 1827 and became abbot of the newly-established monastery of Solesmes in 1837 at the age of 32. His protégé, Cécile Bruyère, later became first abbess of Solesmes' sister house, Saint Cecilia, at the age of 24.[2] This pair of facts hints at the preternatural maturity and enormous energy of the movement to restore Benedictine monasticism in post-revolutionary France, where it seemed nothing could stop the Catholic revival, romantic in spirit and ultramontanist in politics. Dom Prosper Guéranger was that unusual combination of a man of action and a man of letters. Like Nehemiah's description of the rebuilders of Jerusalem—"Those

---

1 Dom Guéranger, quoted in Mary David Totah, OSB, *The Spirit of Solesmes* (Petersham, MA: St. Bede's Publications, 1997), 180.
2 The story is told that when Dom Guéranger was criticized for having chosen such a young nun to be abbess of a new monastery, he replied, with a twinkle in his eye: "Youth is the only fault of which we are automatically cured with the passing of each day."

who carried burdens were laden in such a way that each with one hand labored on the work and with the other held his weapon, and each of the builders had his sword girded at his side while he built" (Neh 4:17–18)—Dom Guéranger founded monastic communities and guided their growth, at the same time battling against a host of contemporary French foes[3] and defending the dogmas of the Immaculate Conception (1854) and papal infallibility as defined by the First Vatican Council (1870).[4]

Guéranger's spiritual vision culminates in the primacy and centrality of the sacred liturgy, the *opus Dei* or work of God to which the monk and nun are especially consecrated, but for which every Christian man, woman, and child has been equipped and set apart in baptism, as a royal priesthood, a holy nation (cf. 1 Pet 2:9). It is thus eminently fitting that he is best known today for his *The Liturgical Year* (*L'Année liturgique*), a leisurely fifteen-volume tour of the feasts and seasons of the Catholic calendar, left unfinished at the time of his death but quickly completed by his disciples, and still in print.[5] On a more scholarly side, the *Institutions liturgiques*, originally published in three volumes (1840, 1841, and 1851) and posthumously republished in four volumes (1878–85) but lamentably not yet translated into English, is a groundbreaking work in every sense, abundantly justifying Dom Guéranger's reputation as the father of the Liturgical Movement.[6] Beginning with the liturgy's apostolic

---

3 Namely, Jansenism, Gallicanism, naturalism, and liberalism.

4 Were Guéranger alive today, he would bitterly regret and repudiate the twin misunderstandings of papal infallibility in the period after the Second Vatican Council, when some people limit the authority of the papacy to an almost non-existent exercise of extraordinary definition in order to justify their moral libertinism, while others extend this authority to any and all papal *dicta et acta* in order to lend support to their abandonment of Catholic Tradition. Guéranger would rightly have regarded both camps as odious.

5 This work is available in print from Loreto Books and St. Bonaventure Publications, and online at http://www.liturgialatina.org/lityear/.

6 For discussion of the original Liturgical Movement and its corruption in the twentieth century, see Peter Kwasniewski, *Noble Beauty, Transcendent Holiness: Why the Modern Age Needs the Mass of Ages* (Kettering, OH: Angelico Press, 2017), 89–133.

foundations, Guéranger offers an account of its organic development that does justice to the prerogatives of the Holy Spirit, who leads the Church into the fullness of truth by inspiring an ever-deeper insight into and an ever more fitting public expression of the mysteries of Christ embodied in and transmitted by the sacramental rites. The copiously detailed historical analysis, the identification and critique of liturgical deviations from the Roman tradition at its best, and the unusual attentiveness to the aesthetic dimension of the liturgy mark the *Institutions liturgiques* as a monument in its field.[7]

If later authors have been in possession of more and better primary data, they have seldom enjoyed Guéranger's intuitive sense of *rectitudo* or rightness, his refreshing common sense in the face of zealots and would-be reformers, his fierce devotion to the life-giving stream of tradition, his willingness to call out heresy,[8] and above all, his profound devotion to the liturgy as a canticle of love offered by the Bride of Christ to her Lord. He was no mere scholar of liturgy delving into archaeological minutiae, much less a pragmatic architect of endlessly rotating pastoral plans, but a man of prayer who ordered his life and the lives of others to the worthy offering of the sacrifice of praise, and who sought to introduce as many of the faithful as possible into a world of marvelous secrets bequeathed to us by Tradition. If we want to *be* Catholic, if we want to think and feel, live and die as Catholics do, we must drink deeply from this pure spring of the inherited liturgy, or else we shall find

---

7 It is therefore nauseating to see Paul VI in 1975 connecting the venerable name of Guéranger with the destruction of the Roman liturgy after the Council: "The new springtime the Church is experiencing today [!] by means of the liturgical renewal is as it were the fruit of that seed which Dom Guéranger worked to scatter with a patient heart and at the price of so many labours" (quoted in Totah, 183, n. 2). One need only read a few dozen pages of *The Liturgical Year* or *Institutions liturgique* to see the stark contrast between the venerable father and his wayward grandchildren.

8 Particularly in his searing chapter "Of the Anti-Liturgical Heresy and the Protestant Reform," parts of which are translated at catholicapologetics.info/modern-problems/newmass/antigy.htm. Some passages from this chapter are discussed in Kwasniewski, *Noble Beauty*, 123–27, 157–59.

ourselves prisoners of some confining human substitute of rational regimentation, be it Jansenist or Bugninian, Gallican or ecumenical. As another Benedictine monk was to point out much later:

> The field of liturgy is itself a *locus theologicus* of inexhaustible wealth, a scattered network, as it were, of doctrinal truths with no systematic ordering. Péguy was right to describe the liturgy as a kind of "relaxed theology." Full of poetry, the *Exultet* arises in the night of the Easter Vigil, and the dogma of the Redemption illumines our understanding with its light, which is none other than the natural splendour of the truth. The *Exultet*, the *Lauda Sion*, the *Dies Irae* are, as it were, chanted doctrine, infusing directly into the soul both light and love. Dom Guéranger once said, in words which were quite surprising at the time, that the liturgy was in fact Tradition in its most powerful and most solemn guise.[9]

The many fine qualities of *The Liturgical Year* and *Institutions liturgiques* are also found in the present book, a succinct and beautiful presentation of the prayers and ceremonies of the traditional Latin Mass. This little work delivers a surprisingly complete exposition of the theology and spirituality of the Holy Sacrifice of the Mass by way of commentary on the texts and gestures of the *usus antiquior* or *Vetus Ordo*. In this way, beyond its author's original intention, it is capable of showing us anew the treasure we have always possessed in this magnificent liturgy, the tragedy of its near extinction in the period after the Second Vatican Council under the myopic ideology of *aggiornamento*, and the immense blessing of its gradual return across the Catholic world, wherever the ideals of the original Liturgical Movement have retained or regained their strength. Consequently, as time goes on, we shall have not less but more and more reason to take up the writings of Dom Guéranger, and we shall discover in him not a relic of the nineteenth century but a prophet of the twenty-first.

---

9 A Benedictine Monk [Dom Gérard Calvet], *The Sacred Liturgy* (Southampton: The Saint Austin Press, 1999), 83.

The value of the present book and others by Guéranger is considerable in a time where there is an absolutely appalling lack of liturgical knowledge and piety. In my career as a teacher of undergraduate and graduate students, I have come to think that this ignorance and, at times, actual inculcation in error explains why it is so difficult initially to make headway in encouraging them to live a *vita liturgica*, that is, a life centered on the sacred liturgy.[10] If all someone has ever known is the "mini-Mass" or "Mass Lite"—that is, the vernacular Pauline paraliturgy, celebrated horizontally in a closed circle, denuded of nearly every sign of the sacred—he will look at you with glazed eyes, not knowing what you could possibly be saying: "Center my life on *what?*" It would be just as easy to sell someone on the merits of the intellectual life when he has never once tasted the joy of philosophy, or to persuade someone of the value of poring over the Great Books when she has only ever skimmed textbooks. When the liturgy is bland, perfunctory, verbose with today's vernacular and mired in today's music, it does not—it *cannot*—stand out as the supreme act of worship, the center of gravity for Christian life, the most special, most important thing we can possibly do in the presence of the thrice-holy God. In short: the single greatest impediment to living a *vita liturgica* is the reformed liturgy, precisely because of its assimilation to a modernity that is anti-sacramental, anti-ritual, anti-religious, anti-transcendent. In attending the new liturgy, one moves progressively into further and further stages of alienation from the true liturgical spirit and its embodiment in authentic tradition. For this alienation, there are but two cures: the immediate and frequent experience of reality, and prayerful, intelligent reflection on what we have encountered. The former happens through firsthand immersion in the traditional liturgy (and for

---

10 See the Second Vatican Council's Constitution on the Sacred Liturgy *Sacrosanctum Concilium* (4 December 1963), §18: "Priests, both secular and religious, who are already working in the Lord's vineyard are to be helped by every suitable means to understand ever more fully what it is that they are doing when they perform sacred rites; they are to be aided to live the liturgical life and to share it with the faithful entrusted to their care."

such immersion there can be no substitute); the latter is provided by competent liturgists like Dom Guéranger, in books like this one.

"Let *nothing* be put before the work of God," Saint Benedict asserts.[11] This sovereign principle of cenobitic monasticism became the foundational principle of Catholicism and Christendom. What have we done instead? As the Israelites repeatedly put their Egypt-craving appetites before the privilege of worshiping the true God, we have put dozens of things before the *opus Dei*: ecumenism, inter-religious dialogue, youth ministry, social work, immigration reform, feminism, new evangelization, you name it—as long as you do not name the Holy Sacrifice of the Mass or the Divine Office. Ironically, even the organization graced with the name *Opus Dei* puts secular work and fellowship before what is properly called the *opus Dei*. The disappearance of Christianity from the West is caused by nothing other than this eclipse of our first duty, our first love. If a spouse betrays a spouse, it does not matter how many children they have, or how big a house, or how much worldly success; the marriage is vitiated at its core, and the rest turns to ashes. The penitential formula "thou art dust, and to dust thou shalt return" could be pronounced as a verdict on the project of contemporary Catholicism, which has abandoned the immortal spirit for the corruptible flesh.

The first step, then, in awakening the soul to the grandeur of the liturgy is nothing other than to lead people to the traditional Mass, where they will experience something strange and uncomfortable, something directed to God and not wrapped up with them, something curiously unmodern and even indifferent to its surroundings, yet obviously utterly in earnest. As Bishop Athanasius Schneider has said, the liturgical reform was an act of violence that has wounded Christ's Mystical Body on earth.[12] For fifty years we have deprived Our Lord of due worship and ourselves of its benefits, with Him as its sole object and we as humble servants of His ineffable mysteries.

---

11 See Saint Benedict, *Rule*, ch. 43.

12 Athanasius Schneider, "The Extraordinary Form and the New Evangelization," first published in English by *Paix Liturgique* in Letter 26, 12 March 2012, and available at a number of places online.

We must not only repair this damage, but, as Aristotle would have it, bend the stick in the opposite direction,[13] cleaving with all our might to inherited forms redolent of the truths and pieties of the Age of Faith. The traditional liturgy of the Church benefits modern man precisely by accentuating much that is profoundly *unmodern*—truths that come to us from the Old Testament, the Apostolic age, the Church of the Fathers, the Middle Ages, every century through which the believing and adoring Bride of Christ has walked, offering up her Lord and herself in the *sacrificium laudis*. Dom Guéranger is an ideal guide in this unfamiliar realm, and we would do well to apprentice ourselves to him, so that we might lose some of our contemporary illiteracy and acquire the learning of the saints.

13 Aristotle, *Nicomachean Ethics*, trans. Roger Crisp (New York: Cambridge University Press, 2000), Bk. 2, ch. 9: "We should drag ourselves in the opposite direction, because we shall arrive at the mean by holding far off from where we would miss the mark, just as people do when straightening warped pieces of wood."

PRELIMINARY NOTICE TO
THIS TRANSLATION

THE WELL-KNOWN TRANSLATOR of the *Liturgical Year* has gone to his rest: but in a twofold sense we may say: *his works follow him.* This his last, and unfinished work, must therefore come to the readers of the *Liturgical Year,* as a loving farewell from him, a memento of him and of his lifelong labours in the cause of Holy Church.

To many, it will be of consoling interest to know that, up to the day of his death, as long as speech was his, Rev. Dom Laurence Shepherd was full of the great passion of his heart—to gain souls to the love of Holy Church. Several times, within even the last month of his painful illness, did he strive to master sinking nature, and once more guide his trembling pen, to tell the faithful something more of the *Bride of Christ,* the Church of God. Those last pages which came from his failing hand close with the word *Lucia,* in the explanation of the *Nobis quoque peccatoribus.* Before the month was out, his friends had poured forth the consoling prayer put on their lips by Mother Church, *Et lux perpetua luceat ei!* Hope had kindled in every heart the reverential confidence that the champion of Holy Church had received the *Corona Justitiae*—had passed to the *Patria Lucis Aeternae.*

Saint Mary's Abbey, Stanbrook
14 June 1885

PREFACE

THE GREAT BISHOP OF POITIERS, Msgr Pie, in his funeral oration on our father, Dom Guéranger, said: "You have long been feasting at a royal board, where you were daily regaled with the most delicate and varied food. Those conferences on the Christian life and virtues, and that incomparable commentary on your Rule—you have no right to keep them to yourselves."

Notwithstanding so pressing an invitation on the part of so competent a judge, as was this devoted friend of our father, we have hesitated long before yielding up to public gaze the secret of our family treasure. It seemed to us that such notes as these would only do for his own sons, eager of paternal instructions and never likely to carp at either the simplicity of the form, or at the incorrectness of the language.

But so very many friends, assiduous readers of Dom Guéranger's *Liturgical Year*, by their repeated solicitations and earnest appeals, have succeeded at length in dissipating our first fears. They are fully aware that they cannot expect to find once more the eminent writer himself, in mere notes, jotted down at the time, almost on the sly, and afterwards hastily put together in a form, the faultiness and inexactitude of which can never be imputed to any one, save to the more or less faithful copyists. But there is one thing they are sure to find in these pages—the teacher and the father, who in intimacy with his friends or his monks, ever with lavish hand, distributed that sure and luminous doctrine which leads souls to God.

We here open our proposed publication, by a short commentary on the ceremonies of Holy Mass, incomplete though we certainly know it to be, in many points, and characterised, as were all our father's conferences, by a total absence of all pretension to erudition: we have not, therefore, presumed to change or add anything. Yet, mere notes, as these are, they seem to us calculated to do good of no little importance.

Thus will the faithful be provided, in this small work, with an efficient means of uniting themselves with the priest in an enlightened manner, and be helped to derive more fruit from their assisting at the Holy Sacrifice of the Mass.

On the welcome accorded to this first attempt at giving publicity to our family treasures, will depend our future decision as to the opportuneness of continuing the proposed series of this *Collection of Notes.*

THE TRADITIONAL
LATIN MASS EXPLAINED

T HE ORDINARY OF THE MASS, (or, as it is called in the Roman Missal, *Ordo Missae*) is the summary of the rubrics and prayers, which are used in the celebration of Mass, and which are observed, without any variation, on all the feasts celebrated by the Church.

We shall never have anything like a full idea of the ceremonies of the Mass, unless we keep referring to what is called a *High Mass* (*Missa Solemnis*), and which is the type of all others. Thus, one would ask, why does the priest say the Epistle at one side of the altar, and the Gospel at the other? Why not read both from the middle? This has no connection with the Holy Sacrifice itself; it is merely an imitation of what is done in a High Mass, in which the deacon has to sing the Gospel on the left, and the subdeacon the Epistle on the right, as we shall explain further on. The priest who celebrates a Mass without deacon and subdeacon, has to take their functions in this instance; and, accordingly, varies his position. We shall continually have to seek in the ceremonies of a High Mass, for the meaning of those of a Low Mass.

The Sacrifice of the Mass is the Sacrifice of the Cross itself; and in it we must see our Lord nailed to the Cross; and offering up his Blood for our sins, to his Eternal Father. And yet we must not expect to find, in the several portions of the Mass, all the detailed circumstances of the Passion, as some authors have pretended to do, when giving us methods for assisting at it.

The priest leaves the sacristy, and goes to the altar, there to offer up the Holy Sacrifice. He is, as the rubric expresses it, *paratus*—that is, he is clad in the sacred vestments, which are appointed for the celebration of the Sacrifice. Having reached the altar, he makes the due reverence before it; that is to say, if the Blessed Sacrament be there, he makes a genuflexion; otherwise, he merely makes a profound inclination. This is the meaning of the rubrics saying: *debita reverentia*.

JUDICA, PSALM 42

Having made the Sign of the Cross, the priest says the antiphon: *Introibo ad altare Dei*, as an introduction to the 42nd Psalm. This antiphon is always said, both before and after the Psalm, which he at once begins: *Judica me Deus*. He says the whole of it, alternately with the ministers. This Psalm was selected on account of the verse *Introibo ad altare Dei*: I will go unto the altar of God. It is most appropriate as a beginning to the Holy Sacrifice. We may remark here, that the Church always selects the Psalms she uses, because of some specal verse which is appropriate to what she does, or to what she wishes to express. The Psalm, of which we are now speaking, was not in the more ancient missals: its usage was established by Pope Saint Pius V, in 1568. When we hear the priest saying this Psalm, we understand to whom it refers: it refers to our Lord, and it is in His Name, that the priest recites it. We are told this by the very first verse: *Ab homine iniquo et doloso erue me*: deliver me from the unjust and deceitful man.

The verse here used as an antiphon, shows us that David was still young when he composed this Psalm; for, after saying, that he is going to the altar of God, he says: *Ad Deum, qui laetificat juventutem meam*: to God, who giveth joy to my youth. He expresses astonishment at his soul being sad; and, at once, cheers himself, by rousing his hope in God; hence, his song is full of gladness. It is on account of the joy which is the characteristic of this Psalm, that Holy Church would have it be omitted in Masses for the dead, in which we are about to pray for the repose of a soul, whose departure from this life leaves us in uncertainty and grief. It is omitted, also, during Passiontide, in which season, the Church is all absorbed in the sufferings of her Divine Spouse; and these preclude all joy.

This 42nd Psalm is an appropriate introduction to the Mass, inasmuch as it in our Lord whom it will bring among us. Who is He that is to be *sent* to the Gentiles, but He that is Light and Truth? David foresaw all this; and, therefore, he uttered the prayer: *Emitte lucem tuam et veritatem tuam*. We take his prayer and make it ours; and we say to our Heavenly Father: send forth Him, who is Thy Light and Thy Truth!

The Psalm having been terminated by the *Gloria Patri*, and the antiphon repeated, the priest asks for God's assistance, saying *Adjutorium nostrum in nomine Domini*: our help is in the name of the Lord. To which the ministers reply: *Qui fecit coelum et terram*: who hath made Heaven and earth. In the Psalm just recited, the priest expressed his ardent desire to possess our Lord, who is Light and Truth: but the very thought, that he—a sinful creature—is about to meet this Lord of his, makes him feel the need he has of help. True—God has willed this meeting; he has even vouchsafed to prescribe it as one of our duties: and yet, notwithstanding, man is continually made to feel his unworthiness and nothingness. Before going further in the Holy Sacrifice, he is determined to humble himself, and confess that he is a sinner. He encourages himself to this, by making the Sign of the Cross, and imploring God's aid. He then begins the avowal of his sins.

CONFITEOR

Holy Church here makes use of the formula of confession, which she has drawn up; it probably dates from the eighth century. We are not allowed to make the slightest change in the words. It has

3

this prerogative, in common with all the other *sacramentals*—that its recitation produces the forgiveness of venial sins, provided we be contrite for them. Thus it is, that God, in His infinite goodness, has provided us with other means, over and above the Sacrament of Penance, whereby we may be cleansed from our venial sins: He, for this end, inspired His Church to give us her *sacramentals*.

The priest, as we were saying, begins the confession; and, first of all, he accuses himself to God. But, he is not satisfied with that—he as good as says: "I not only desire to confess my sins to God, but to all the saints; in order that they may join their prayers with mine, and obtain pardon for me." Therefore, he immediately adds: "I confess to the Blessed Mary ever Virgin." Not that he has ever committed any offence against this holy mother; but he has sinned in her sight; and the very thought of it urges him to make his sins known to her also. He does the same to the glorious Saint Michael, the great archangel, who is appointed to watch over our souls, especially at the hour of death. In like manner, he confesses to Saint John the Baptist, who was so dear to our Lord, and was His precursor. Lastly, he desires to own his sins to Saints Peter and Paul, the two Princes of the Apostles. Certain religious orders have permission to add the name of their patriarch or founder. Thus, the Benedictines insert the name of Saint Benedict; the Dominicans, Saint Dominic; the Franciscans, Saint Francis. After mentioning these and all the saints, he would have even the faithful, who are present, know that he is a sinner; and he therefore says to them: *And to you, Brethren!* because, as he is now humbling himself on account of his sins, he not only accuses himself before those who are glorified in God, but moreover, before those his fellow mortals who are there visibly present, near the sanctuary. And not satisfied with declaring himself to be a sinner, he adds in what way he has sinned; and confesses, that it is by all the three ways, wherein men commit sin, namely, by thought, word, and deed: *cogitatione, verbo, et opere.* Then wishing to express, that he has thus sinned and through his own free will, be utters these words: *Mea culpa, mea culpa, mea maxima culpa*: through my fault, through my fault, through my most grievous fault. And, that he may, like the publican of the Gospel, outwardly testify his inward repentance, he thrice strikes his breast, whilst saying those words. Conscious of the need he has of pardon, he once more turns towards Mary and all the saints, as likewise to the faithful who are present, begging that they will all pray for him. In reference to this formula of confession, which has been established by our Holy Mother the Church, it may be well to remind our readers, that it would, of itself, suffice for one who was in danger of death, and unable to make a more explicit confession.

The ministers answer the priest by wishing him the grace of God's Mercy; they express their wish under the form of prayer, during which he, the priest, remains bowed down, and answers: *Amen*.

But, the ministers themselves stand in need of God's pardon; and, therefore, they repeat the same formula as the priest, for the confession of their sins; only, instead of saying: *Et vobis, fratres*, and to you, brethren, they address the priest, and call him father: *Et tibi, Pater*.

It is never allowable to change anything which Holy Church has prescribed for the celebration of the Mass. Hence, in the *Confiteor*, the ministers must always use the simple words: *Et tibi, Pater; Et te, Pater*; they must add no further title, not even were they serving the pope's Mass.

As soon as the ministers have finished the confession formula, the priest says the same prayer for them, as they had previously made for him; and they, also, respond to it by an *Amen*. A sort of blessing then follows: *Indulgentiam, etc.*, whereby the priest asks, both for himself and his brethren, pardon and forgiveness of their sins; he makes the Sign of the Cross, and uses the word *nobis* and not *vobis*, for he puts himself on an equality with his ministers, and takes his share in the prayer that is said for all.

The confession having been made, the priest again bows down, but not so profoundly as he did during the *Confiteor*. He says: *Deus, tu conversus vivificabis nos*: Thou, O God, with one look, wilt give us life; to which the ministers answer: *Et plebs tua laetabitur in te*: And thy people will rejoice in thee. Then—*Ostende nobis, Domine, misericordiam tuam*: Show unto us Thy Mercy, O Lord; *Et salutare tuum da nobis*: and grant us the Saviour whom Thou hast prepared for us. The practice of reciting these versicles is very ancient. The last gives us the words of David, who, in his 84th Psalm, is praying for the coming of the Messias. In the Mass, before the Consecration, we await the coming of our Lord, as they, who lived before the Incarnation, awaited the promised Messias. By that word mercy, which is here used by the Prophet, we are not to understand the goodness of God; but, we ask of God, that He will vouchsafe to send us Him, who in His Mercy and His Salvation, that is to say, the Saviour, by whom Salvation is to come upon us. These few words of the Psalm take us back in spirit, to the season of Advent, when we are unceasingly asking for Him who is to come.

After this, the priest asks of God, that He would vouchsafe to grant his prayer: *Domine, exaudi orationem meam*: Lord, hear my prayer. The ministers continue, as though in his name: *Et clamor meus ad te veniat*: and let my cry come unto Thee. The priest salutes the people, saying: *Dominus vobiscum*: the Lord be with you. It is as though he were taking leave of them, now that the solemn moment is come for him to ascend the altar, and, like Moses, enter into the cloud. The ministers answer him in the name of the people: *Et cum spiritu tuo*: and with thy spirit.

Whilst going up to the altar, the priest says *Oremus*: he stretches out his hands, and joins them again. As often as he uses this word, he observes the same ceremony. The reason is, that it immediately precedes some prayer which he is going to make; and, when we pray, we raise our hands up to God, who is in Heaven, and to whom we are about to speak. It was thus that our Blessed Lord prayed on the Cross. In the prayer, which the priest says, whilst ascending the altar steps, he uses the plural, because he is not alone; for the deacon and subdeacon go up together with him, and minister to him. The thought which is uppermost in the priest's mind, at this solemn moment is, to be all pure; for, as he says, he is entering into the Holy of Holies: *Ad Sancta Sanctorum*, meaning to express, by this Hebrew superlative, the importance of the act which he is going to fulfil. He prays, therefore, that his sins, as well as those of his ministers, may be taken away. The nearer we approach to God, the more we feel the slightest sin to be an intolerable blot upon our soul; so that the priest redoubles his prayer, that God would cleanse him from his sins. He has already prayed this *merciful* Lord to *turn* and give him life; *Deus tu conversus vivificabis nos. Ostende nobis Domine misericordiam tuam.* But, having drawn nearer to that God, his fear increases, and his desire of pardon is more ardent; he repeats this same prayer again now whilst going up the altar steps. Having reached the altar, he puts his hands upon it, first joined, and then separated, so that he may kiss it. This kissing the altar is prompted by a sentiment of respect for the saints' relics, which are there. Again, another prayer for pardon of his sins: in it, he says: *peccata mea*: my sins; although he began it by: *Oramus Te, Domine*: we beseech thee, O Lord; nor is there any inadvertency in this; for, all those who assist at the Holy Sacrifice should entertain, for the priest, a sentiment of filial respect, and pray with and for him.

INCENSING THE ALTAR

The altar represents our Lord Jesus Christ. The saints' relics which are there, remind us that the saints are His members. For, having assumed our human nature, He not only suffered His Passion, triumphed in His Resurrection, and entered into His glory by the Ascension—but He, also, founded the Church upon earth, and this Church is His mystical Body; He is its Head, and the saints are its members. From this point of view, then, our Lord has not the fullness of His mystical Body without His saints; and it is for this reason, that the saints, who are reigning with Him in glory, are united with Him, in the altar, which represents Him.

The priest, having finished the prayer, which he said bowing down, and his hands joined on the altar, prepares for its Incensing. Twice will this take place during the Holy Sacrifice, and both times with much solemnity, out of respect for our Lord, who is signified by the altar, as we have already said. Nevertheless, the priest does not recite any prayer during the first incensing; he merely thurifies every portion of the altar, in such wise as that the whole of it is thus honoured. We learn from the Book of Leviticus, that incense was used, at a very early period, in the divine worship. The blessing, which the priest gives it in the Mass, raises this production of nature to the supernatural order. Holy Church has borrowed this ceremony from Heaven itself; where Saint John witnessed it. In his Apocalypse, he saw an angel, standing, with a golden censer, near the altar, on which was the Lamb, with four-and-twenty elders around him (Apoc. 8:3). He describes this angel to us, as offering to God the prayers of the saints, which are symbolised by the incense. Thus, our Holy Mother the Church, the faithful Bride of Christ, wishes to do as Heaven does; and taking advantage of the veil of its mysterious secrets being even thus partially raised up by the Beloved Disciple, she borrows, for our earth's imitation, the tribute of honour thus paid, yonder above, to the glory of her Spouse. At this part of the Mass, the altar alone, and the priest, are thurified; the incensing of the choir is reserved for the second time of the ceremony, which is at the Offertory. It is one of the customs of the Church to expose, on the altar, images and relics of the saints, which then are incensed at the same time.

INTROIT

The ceremony of the incensing completed, the priest says the Introit. Formerly, this was not done. The *Ordo* of Saint Gregory tells us, that the priest vested in the *Secretarium*, and then went to the altar, preceded by the Cross and torches; during which time, the choir sang the Introit, which was longer than we now have it, for the entire Psalm was sung, and not merely one or two of its verses, with the *Gloria Patri*, as at present.

In like manner, it was the choir alone that took the remaining portions, which were to be sung during the Mass. The custom of the priest's reciting these several portions, originated with that of

Low Mass, which custom was, at last, introduced into High Masses. These remarks will explain how it is, that the ancient missals differ considerably from those which are now in use. They simply contain the prayers: Collects, Secrets, Postcommunions, Prefaces, and the Canon. They were called *sacramentaries*. Whatever was sung by the choir was inserted in the *antiphonarium*, which now goes under the name of *Gradual*. (Most of the chanted portions of the Mass are, really, nothing more than antiphons; only, they have more notes than what ordinary antiphons have.) In more modern times, ever since Low Masses were introduced, our missals contain everything that used, formerly, to be sung by the choir; as also the Epistles and Gospels.

Both the priest and the choir make the Sign of the Cross at the beginning of the Introit, because it is considered as the opening of the readings. In Masses for the dead, the priest makes the Cross over the missal only.

KYRIE

Next follows the *Kyrie*, which, at a High Mass, is said at the same side of the altar, where the Introit was read. The priest is accompanied by his ministers, who do not go to the middle of the altar, until he himself does; meanwhile, they stand behind him, on the steps. In a Low Mass, the priest says the *Kyrie*, in the middle. This prayer is a cry of entreaty, whereby the Church sues for mercy from the Blessed Trinity. The first three invocations are addressed to the Father, who is Lord: *Kyrie, Eleison*; Lord, have mercy. The following three are addressed to Christ, the Son incarnate: *Christe, eleison*. The last three are addressed to the Holy Ghost, who is Lord, together with the Father and the Son; and therefore, we say to Him also: *Kyrie, eleison*. The Son, too, is equally Lord, with the Father and the Holy Ghost: but, Holy Church here gives Him the title of Christ, because of the relation this word bears to the Incarnation. The choir, too, takes up the same nine invocations; and sings them. Formerly, it was the practice, in many churches, to intersperse them with words, which were sung to the same melody as the invocations themselves, as we find in several old missals. The Missal of Saint Pius V did away, almost entirely, with these *Kyrie*, called, on account of these popular additions, *Farsati*, (in French, *farcis*). When the pope celebrates a Solemn Mass, the singing of the *Kyrie* is continued during the act of homage which is paid him on his throne: but this is an exception to the present observance throughout the Church. The three invocations, each repeated thrice over (as now practised), are like a telling us of our union, here below, with the *nine* choirs of angels, who sing, in Heaven, the *glory* of the Most High. This union prepares us to join them in the hymn which is now to follow, and which these blessed spirits brought down to this our earth.

GLORIA IN EXCELSIS

Then the priest has to intone the *Gloria in Excelsis Deo,* he goes to the middle of the altar; extends his arms at first, and then joins his hands together; but, neither here, nor at the intonation of the *Credo*, does he raise up his eyes. At the close of the hymn, he makes the Sign of the Cross, because there is pronounced the name of Jesus, who, together with the Holy Ghost, is in the glory of God the Father; and thus mention is made of the Blessed Trinity. This hymn is one of the most ancient in the Church's collection. There has been an attempt made (Msgr Cousseau, Bishop of Angoulême) to prove that it was composed by Saint Hilary. But there are really no grounds for such an assertion. One thing is certain—that this hymn dates from the earliest days of the Church, and that it is to be found in all the missals of the Eastern Churches. Nothing can exceed the beauty of its expressions. It is not a long composition, like, for example, the Preface, in which Holy Church always begins by some doctrinal teaching, and then turns to prayer: here, on the contrary, all is enthusiasm and fervent language of the soul. The angels themselves intoned the hymn; and the Church, inspired as she is, by the Holy Ghost, continues the words of the angels.

Let us dwell upon the words of this magnificent canticle. *Gloria in excelsis Deo! et in terra, pax hominibus bonae voluntatis*: Glory be to God in the highest Heavens; and peace on earth to men of good will; to men that are beloved of God. These are the words of the angels: to God, be glory; to men, who, heretofore, were all children of wrath, the peace and blessing of God. In this the opening of the hymn, it speaks to God, without distinction of Persons; and Holy Mother Church, after the example of the angels, takes up, at first, the same tone; and thus continues: *Laudamus te*: we praise Thee; for praise is due to Thee, and we offer it unto Thee. *Benedicimus te*: we bless Thee; that is to say, we offer Thee thanksgiving, in return for Thy benefits. *Adoramus te*: we adore Thee, O Infinite Majesty! *Glorificamus te*: we give glory to Thee, for that Thou hast created and redeemed us. The bare addressing these several expressions to God, with the intention of praising Him, thanking Him, adoring Him, and glorifying Him, is a perfect prayer and praise; such is the intention of the Church; let it be ours, and we shall not need to go in search of any higher meaning to our words. *Gratias agimus tibi propter magnam gloriam tuam*: we give thee thanks for thy great glory. The better to take in the deep meaning of these few words, let us remember that God vouchsafes to make it a glory to Himself to bestow His favours upon us. The greatest of these is the Incarnation; and the Incarnation is his greatest glory. Hence, the Church might well say to Him: we give thee thanks, because of Thy great glory; The homage paid by the Word Incarnate, even in what might be thought the least of his adorations, procures more glory to the Divine Majesty, than all created beings, unitedly, could do. Truly, therefore, the Incarnation is the *great glory of God*. And we His creatures give Him thanks for it; because if the Son of God became Incarnate, it was for us, it was because of us, that He did so. Yea, it is for us, that Thou, O God, achievedst the mystery which gives Thee the greatest glory: it is most just, then, that we thank Thee for it: *Gratias agimus tibi, propter magnam gloriam tuam! Domine Deus, Rex coelestis, Deus Pater omnipotens*: O Lord God, Heavenly King, God the Father Almighty. Here, the Church addresses herself directly to the Father.

Previously, she was intent on the Unity which is in the Godhead; she now thinks of the Trinity; and seeing, first of all, the divine Person who is the Principle and source of the other Two, she exclaims *Deus Pater omnipotens!* God, Father Almighty! Then she turns to her Divine Spouse. She can never tire speaking of Him; and almost all the rest of the canticle is addressed to Him. She sings the Incarnate Son of God, and she calls Him Lord: *Domine, Fili unigenite*: Lord, the Only Begotten Son! She also calls Him by the human name which he received as creature: *Jesu Christe!* But, she does not forget that He is God; she loudly proclaims it, saying: *Domine **Deus**, Agnus Dei, Filius Patris!* Yes, her Spouse is God; he is, too, the Lamb of God, as Saint John declared Him to the people; and, finally, He is Son of the Father. In her delighted love, Holy Church gives her Spouse every title she can think of; she enumerates His glories; it is a joy to her to announce them all in turn. Among these titles, she gives Him that of *Lamb of God*; but she seems to falter a moment, before adding what is the sad consequence of that title—namely, that He had to take the world's sins upon Himself. She must, first, speak again of His magnificence; she calls Him *Filius Patris*; and this said, she takes heart, and sings out to her Spouse, that, being the Lamb, He has humbled Himself so low, as to take upon Himself the sins of the world: *Qui tollis peccata mundi.* Who takest, and takest away, the sins of the world. Thou hast deigned to redeem us by Thy Blood; now, therefore, that Thou art in glory, at the right hand of Thy Father, abandon us not, but have mercy upon us: *Miserere nobis!* She no longer hesitates to say those words; she repeats them, for they tell us where our strength lies: *Qui tollis peccata mundi.* The Lamb of God, the Son of the Father, taking away our defilements and our sins, what have we to fear? Is it not this that makes us strong? The Church is thus minded. She tells and retells the glorious truth first, she asks for mercy and then, she beseeches Him to attend to the prayer of His Bride: *Suscipe deprecationem nostram.* Behold us here assembled for the Sacrifice; receive, then, our humble prayer.

After having thus spoken, Holy Church contemplates her divine Spouse throned in the highest Heavens: *Qui sedes ad dexteram Patris*:

Who sittest at the right hand of the Father. Just before, she was complacently looking at Him as the Lamb of God, who had taken on Himself the sins of the whole world; she now advances higher, and goes even to the Father's right hand, where she beholds Him who is the object of her adoration and praise. There, she reaches the very Being of God; there, she pays her homage to all Holiness, all Justice, all Plenitude, all Greatness, as she is now going to proclaim. But, first, she repeats her cry for mercy: *Miserere nobis!* Have mercy on us, for Thou hast redeemed us! *Tu solus Sanctus; Tu solus Dominus; Tu solus Altissimus, Jesu Christe*: Thou alone art Holy; Thou alone art Lord; Thou alone art most High, O Christ Jesus! Thus, in this canticle, Holy Church perseveres in her endeavours to reach her divine Spouse; each one of her exclamations is like an attempt to be with Him. She thinks of her own necessities; she thinks of Him; she is all enthusiasm. She no sooner mentions His Name, than she must tell all His Perfections; not one must be forgotten. She dwells on His Name, because He is her Spouse; she praises Him, and glorifies Him, and calls Him the alone God, the alone Lord, the alone Most High. She adds, however: *Cum Sancto Spiritu, in gloria Dei Patris*; together with the Holy Ghost, in the glory of God the Father. Thus, she mentions each of the Three Persons of the Blessed Trinity and the praise she gives to Christ, by calling Him *alone Holy, alone Lord, alone Most High*, applies also to the other two Persons, since the Father and the Holy Ghost cannot be separated from the Son, and, like Him, They are *alone Holy, alone Lord, alone Most High*: and no one is *Holy*, no one is *Lord*, no one is *Most High*, except the great God himself.

In this magnificent canticle, everything is, at once, grand and simple. Holy Church is in admiration at the thought of her divine Spouse. She began with the *Kyrie*; then, the hymn of the angels followed; she took up *their* song, and continued it; and the same Spirit that spoke, through the angels, to the shepherds, taught the Church how to worthily close the canticle.

COLLECT

The *Gloria* being finished, the priest kisses the altar; and, turning towards the people, says *Dominus vobiscum*. He has once already addressed his ministers with this salutation; but he was then at the foot of the altar; it was a sort of farewell; for, when he was just about entering into the cloud, he seemed loath to leave the faithful people, until he had spoken one word, at least, of affection to them that had been praying together with him. But, now, the Church has a different motive for using these two words; and it is, that she may gain the people's attention to the Collect which the priest is going to address to God—in other words, to the prayer in which he sums up the desires of the faithful, and presents them under the form of a petition. The word *Collect* comes from the Latin *colligere*, which means to bring together things previously existing apart. The importance of the Collect is great. Hence, Holy Mother Church urges us to listen to it with all respect and devotion. According to monastic usage, the choir bows down profoundly while the priest recites it: in cathedral chapters, the canons turn towards the altar.

When the Collect is finished, the choir answers *Amen*; that is to say, Yes, that is what we pray for, and we assent to everything that has been said. This first prayer of the Mass is also recited at Vespers, Lauds, and (in the monastic rite) at Matins; the Roman Breviary only says it at the Christmas Matins, before the Midnight Mass. It is not said at Prime, because that portion of the office was of a later institution; neither is it said at Compline, which is considered as night prayers, and received its liturgical form from Saint Benedict. It is said at Tierce, Sext, and None. All this shows us what importance the Church attaches to the Collect, which, so to say, characterises the day; and this explains why it is preceded by the *Dominus vobiscum*, which is as though the priest said to the people: Be all attention, for what is now going to be said, is of the greatest importance. Moreover, the priest, when here saying the *Dominus vobiscum*, turns towards the people, which he did not do when he was at the foot of the altar. But having now ascended to it, and having received the peace of the Lord by kissing the altar, he announces the same to the assembly, to whom, opening his arms, he says: *Dominus vobiscum*. The people reply: *Et cum spiritu tuo*. Then the priest, feeling that the people are one with him, says: *Oremus*; Let us pray.

The *Pax vobis* said here by prelates, instead of *Dominus vobiscum*, is a very ancient usage. It was the customary salutation of the Jews. The words of the *Gloria: Pax hominibus bonae voluntatis* prompted its being used at this part of the Mass. There is every reason for believing, that, in the early Ages, every priest used the formula of *Pax vobis*. It is the same with several of the pontifical ceremonies. Thus, for instance, every priest, used, formerly, to put on the maniple at the moment of his going up to the altar, as a prelate now does. Later on, it was found easier to put it on in the sacristy; this took the place of the ancient practice, the which is now reserved to prelates alone. As the *Pax vobis* is suggested by the *Gloria*, it is not said when the Mass, which is being said, excludes that hymn: in which case, the *Dominus vobiscum* is substituted.

The priest should stretch out his arms, whilst saying the Collect. Herein, he imitates the ancient manner of praying, used by the first Christians. As our Lord had His arms extended on the Cross, and so prayed for us—the early Christians had the practice of praying in that same attitude.

This ancient usage has been transmitted to us, in an especially emphatic way, by the paintings of the catacombs, which always represent prayer as being made in that attitude: hence, the name of *Orantes*, given to those figures. It is by this means, as also by the writings of the Holy Fathers, that many details regarding the usages of the primitive times have been handed down to memory, which, otherwise, would have been lost.

In the East, the practice of praying with outstretched arms is universal; in our western countries, it has become very rare, and is only used on special occasions. We might say, that publicly, it is only the priest who prays in that attitude, for he represents our Lord, who offered a prayer of infinite worth whilst hanging on the Cross; He offered it to His Eternal Father.

EPISTLE

After the Collect, and the other prayers, which are frequently added under the name of Commemorations, there follows the Epistle, which is, almost always, taken from the Epistles of one or other of the Apostles, although, occasionally, from some other book of the Holy Scriptures. The custom of reading only one Epistle in the Mass, is not of the number of those which were in use in the primitive Church; yet it dates back at least a thousand years. In the Early Ages, there was read, first, a lesson from the Old Testament; after which, followed some passage selected from the apostolic writings. At present, it is the Epistle alone that is read, excepting on Ember Days and certain ferias. The practice of reading lessons from the Old Testament during Mass, ceased when the missal was drawn up in its present form, and which contains the whole of what is said at Mass, both by the priest and by the choir; and, on that account, is called a *Full Missal*. An ancient missal, called a *Sacramentary*, contained nothing, as we have already stated, beyond the prayers, the Prefaces, and the Canon. All the rest was to be looked for in the antiphonary, the Bible, and the Evangeliarium. We have been losers by the change; for each Mass had its proper Preface; whereas, now, the number of these liturgical compositions is reduced to a minimum. The same method was observed in the Divine Office, since, in those times, there were no breviaries; and each choir had to be supplied with a Psaltery, Hymnary, Bible, Passional, which related the Acts of the Saints, and a Homily Book, which contained the Sermons of the Holy Fathers.

For a long period after that, the first Sunday of Advent retained its privilege of having two Epistles in the Mass. At last, it, also, was to have but one. The Office of this Sunday was, however, treated with a special consideration, and has retained, more faithfully than most others, the ancient usages. Thus, though a semidouble, the Suffrages are not to be said upon it; nor, indeed, during the whole period up to the Epiphany. The Suffrages do not date beyond the eleventh century; previously there were none.

Thus everything in the Holy Sacrifice proceeds with order: the priest has, first of all, expressed the desires and petitions of the assembled faithful—Holy Church has spoken through him. We shall soon be hearing the words of our divine Master, in the Gospel; but we are to be prepared for that, by the word of his servant; this was done in the Epistle. So that, we first have the Prophet, then the Apostle, and, at length, our Lord Himself.

GRADUAL

Between the Epistle and the Gospel, we have the Gradual. It consists of a responsory and its versicle. Formerly, the whole responsory was repeated both before and after the versicle, in the way now used with the brief responsories; only, the responsory was exceedingly rich in notes. The Gradual is really the most musical piece in the whole liturgy; and, as the rendering of it requires great skill, there were never more than two chanters permitted to sing it. When about to sing it, they went to the ambo, which was a sort of marble pulpit, placed in the church; and it was on account of the *steps*, which led to the ambo, that this portion of the chant got the name of *Gradual*; just as the Gradual Psalms were those which the Jews used to sing whilst ascending the *steps* of the temple.

ALLELUIA — TRACT

The Gradual is followed by the *Alleluia*—or, if the season require it, by the *Tract*. The *Alleluia* is repeated after the manner of a responsory; it is then followed by a verse; which having been said, the Alleluia is sung a third time. This, by excellence, the chant of the praise of God, deserved to have a place in the Mass. There is something so joyous, and, at the same time, so mysterious about it, that during penitential seasons—that is, from Septuagesima to Easter—it is not to be said.

During those seasons, it is replaced by the *Tract*. The Tract takes up the attention of the faithful during the time required for the several ceremonies, when the deacon, after having asked the priest's blessing, goes in procession to the ambo of the Gospel, and prepares to herald the Word of God. The Tract is composed, sometimes of an entire Psalm, or nearly so—as we have for the first Sunday of Lent; but, generally, it gives only a few verses. These verses, which are sung to a rich and characteristic melody, follow each other without any refrain or repetition: and it is because of their being thus sung without any break, that they are called by this name of *Tract*.

SEQUENCE

On certain solemnities, there is added to the *Alleluia* or *Tract*, what is called the *Sequence (Sequentia)*. It was added to the chant of the Mass long after the time of Saint Gregory; the addition was made some time about the ninth century. It received the name of *Sequence*, that is to say, sequel, because it originally consisted of certain words adapted to the notes which form a sequel to the word Alleluia, and which were called *Sequentia*, even before the introduction of the *Sequence*.

It is called, also, the *Prose (Prosa)* because originally, it bore no resemblance either to the metrical hymns composed by ancient writers, nor to cadenced rhythms, which appeared later on. It was a real piece of prose, which was sung in the manner we have described, as a way of putting words to the pneuma of the *Alleluia*. By degrees, however, it partook of the character of a hymn. The Sequence thus added to the solemnity of the liturgy; and, whilst it was being sung, the bells were rung, as now, and the organ was played. There was a Sequence for every feast, and, therefore, for the Sundays during Advent. In the Roman Missal drawn up by order of Saint Pius V, only four of the Sequences were retained. These four are, the *Victimae Paschali*, which is the most ancient of all, and was followed as the model of the rest; the *Veni Sancte Spiritus*, the *Lauda Sion*, and the *Dies irae*. Later on, there was added the *Stabat Mater*. The monastic missal has also the *Laeta dies*, for the feast of Saint Benedict; it is a composition of the sixteenth century.

GOSPEL

Whilst the choir is singing these several pieces, the deacon takes the Book of the Gospels, and puts it upon the altar, because the altar represents our Lord; and he thus signifies the identity existing between the Word of God, which is heard in the Gospel, and Christ Jesus. The priest does not incense the book, but he blesses the incense—an act, which is not permitted to the deacon. The incense having been blessed, the deacon kneels upon the top step of the altar, and says the prayer *Munda cor meum*. In that prayer, he asks of God, that his heart and his lips may be purified, to the end that he may worthily proclaim the Holy Gospel. He there alludes to the coal of fire, with which a seraph touched the lips of the Prophet Isaias, in order to purify him, and fit him to make known the inspirations received from the Holy Ghost (Isa. 6:5–7). This same prayer is also said at private Masses, by the priest. After the prayer, the deacon takes the book from the altar; and, kneeling before the priest, asks for a blessing, because he is going to read: *Jube, Domne, benedicere*; Please, Father, give me a blessing. In a private Mass, the priest asks the blessing of God, saying: *Jube, Domine, benedicere!* and then he answers in the words of the blessing, making such changes as are necessary for the applying them to himself. Having received the blessing, the deacon kisses the hand of the priest, who, for this purpose, should place his hand on the Book of the Gospels, which he thus virtually gives to the deacon, commissioning him to read it in his name.

A procession is then formed towards the Gospel-ambo; and there the deacon begins with this solemn expression: *Dominus vobiscum*. It is the only occasion on which the deacon is allowed to use these words: and his present use of them is equivalent to his preparing the faithful; as though he said to them: You are about to hear the Word of God, the eternal Word: it is a great grace for you all: may, then, the Lord be with you! May he enlighten you, and nourish you with His Word! The people answer him, saying: *Et cum spiritu tuo.* Then, the deacon announces the title of the passage he is going to give them: he tells it them in these words: *Initium,* or *Sequentia sancti Evangelii*; and whilst saying this, he makes the Sign of the Cross upon the book, and at the place where begins the text of the Gospel. He, at the same time, signs himself on the forehead, the lips, and the breast, asking, in virtue of the Cross, which is the source of all grace, that he may always have the Gospel in his heart, and on his lips, and that he may never be ashamed of it. He then takes the thurible, and incenses the book three times; whilst the faithful, in answer to the announcement of the Good Tidings, give thanks and glory to our Lord Jesus Christ, whose Word is now going to be heard: *Gloria tibi, Domine.*

It is now time to sing the Holy Gospel. The deacon joins his hands; but does not lean them on the book, as that would be too great a familiarity with an object so sacred as is the book, which contains the expression of the Eternal Word. The deacon having completed what he had to sing, the subdeacon takes the open book to the celebrant, who kisses the first words of the sacred text, saying: *Per evangelica dicta deleantur nostra delicta*; May our sins be wiped away by these words of the Gospel. In this formula (which is sometimes used as one of the blessings at Matins), we find a species of rhyme, which denotes a medieval origin. Meanwhile, the deacon turns towards the priest, in whose name he has been singing the Gospel; and, taking the thurible, thrice honours him with incense. The priest is the only one to receive this honour at this portion of the liturgy.

The priest, who says Mass without deacon and subdeacon, should, when he reads the Gospel, so place the missal, that he himself shall be somewhat turned towards the North. It is the same with the deacon—he stands facing the North when he sings the Gospel—because, according to the word of the Prophet Jeremias (1:14) *From the North, shall all evil break forth upon all the inhabitants of the Land.* It is for the same mysterious reason, that in the Baptism of adults, the catechumen is put, so as to face the North, when uttering his renunciation of Satan. Formerly, in the larger churches, there were erected two ambos, or pulpits: one for the Epistle, and the other for the Gospel. At present, we do not find these two ambos, except in the two churches at Rome—Saint Clement and Saint Laurence-outside-the-walls. They were used, also, in Saint Paul's, before its restoration. It was at the ambo, that was placed the Paschal Candle, during the forty days preceding the feast of the Ascension.

We should notice the difference, wherewith the Church would have the Epistle and the Gospel announced in the Mass. As to the Epistle, it is merely preceded by the subdeacon's saying whence is taken the passage, which he is going to sing; whereas, the Gospel is always preceded by the words: *Dominus vobiscum.* The reason is, that in the Epistle, it is but the servant that speaks to us; but, in the Gospel, it is the word of the Master himself, which we are about to hear; and, therefore, a means is taken for exciting the attention of the faithful. It is only at the end of the priest's reading of the Gospel, that there is answered: *Laus tibi, Christe*: because, formerly, the celebrant read nothing of what was sung by others; the Gospel was of this number, and he merely listened to it. In Masses for the Dead, the deacon does not ask the priest's blessing, when about to sing the Gospel. As the asking such a blessing is, more or less, a ceremony expressive of Joy, it is omitted, because of the sadness and mourning which accompany a Requiem Mass. Neither are torches borne at the ambo; nor does the priest kiss the book at the end of the Gospel. For the same reason, the deacon does not kiss the priest's hand, after having taken the book from off the altar.

CREDO

The Gospel is followed by the *Credo.* The object proposed by the recitation of the *Credo* is, to lead the faithful to confess the Faith; and since their Faith is based upon the Holy Gospel, the *Credo* comes immediately after the sacred text has been read. It is but right, that the faithful should utter this profession of faith against the heresies that have been broached. The *Credo* is to be said, not only on all Sundays, but, moreover, on the feasts of the Apostles, who preached the faith; on the feasts of Doctors, who defended it; on the feast of Saint Mary Magdalene, who was the first to believe the Resurrection, announced it to the Apostles, and thus became an Apostle to the Apostles; on the feasts of the Holy Angels, because allusion is made to them, in these words: *Maker of Heaven and earth, and of all things visible and invisible*; on the feasts of the Blessed Virgin, because the *Credo* also speaks of our Lady; (but it is omitted in Votive Masses). It is said also on the feast of the Dedication of a Church, and on patronal feasts, because it is supposed, that, on both those days, there will be a large concourse of people; and, it is on that account, that it is said on the feast of Saint John the Baptist, should it fall on a Sunday; for, otherwise, it is not said, because Saint John came before the Mysteries were accomplished, and because there is no mention made of him in the Symbol. The *Credo* is said likewise when a church possesses a large or important relic of the saint whose feast occurs, and on which, it is taken for granted, many faithful will assist at the services.

The Symbol recited during the Mass, is not that of the Apostles—it is that of Nicaea; or, if we would speak with full precision, we should call it the Symbol of Nicaea and Constantinople, inasmuch as the entire article referring to the Holy Ghost was added in the first Council of Constantinople against Macedonius.

Until the eleventh century, the *Credo* was not thus publicly said in the churches at Rome. Saint Henry, Emperor of Germany, when visiting Rome, was surprised at not hearing the *Credo* during the Mass. He spoke on the subject to the then reigning pontiff, Benedict VIII. The pontiff told him, that the Church at Rome gave, in this, an indication of the purity of her faith, and that she had no need to express her rejection of errors, which had never been harboured within her walls. However, shortly after the Emperor's remark, it was decided, that the *Credo* should be said, in the churches in Rome, on Sundays; for that confession of faith would become all the more solemn, by its being promulgated from the very Chair of Saint Peter.

The Nicene Symbol is longer than that of the Apostles, which, nevertheless, contains all the truths of faith; but, as heresies have gradually sprung up, it was found necessary to give further development to such of the articles as were attacked; and thus, the several heresies were pointedly condemned, each one as it appeared. This Symbol contains everything that we have to believe, for we say, in one of the articles: *I believe the Church*; and hence, by believing all that the Holy Church believes, we possess everything that she has adopted, and everything she has declared to be the truth, in the Councils of Nicaea and Constantinople, as also in all the others which followed.

The Symbol used in the Mass begins thus: *Credo in unum Deum*. I believe in one God. The Apostles had not made use of the word *unum*; there was nothing, at that period, to make such an insertion necessary. It was at the Council of Nicaea, that the Church deemed it needful to add that word, in order to maintain the affirmation of the Divine Unity, at the same time that the Trinity of Persons was expressed, which was directed against the Arians. But why do we say: I believe *in* one God? Why use the preposition *in*? It is of the greatest importance, as a moment's reflection will show. What is Faith, but a movement of the soul towards God? That Faith which is united with charity, that living faith placed by Holy Church in the hearts of her children, tends of its very nature towards God, ascends and raises itself up to Him, *Credo in Deum*.

There are two ways of knowing God. A man who sees all things of which the universe is composed—the earth with its numberless productions; the firmament studded with stars, in the midst of which the sun reigns supreme in dazzling splendour, and completes its revolutions in so marvellous a manner—a man, I say, beholding such wonders arranged with so great order and perfection, cannot help recognising that *Some-One* has achieved all that; this is what is called a rational truth. If he failed to come to such a conclusion, he would show a total want of intellect, and would be but on a par with brute beasts to whom understanding has not been given, since they are irrational creatures. This is what is meant by knowing God by reason; we see Creation, and we thence conclude that it is the very work of God Himself. But when we talk of knowing God as the Father, as the Son, and as the Holy Ghost—there is absolutely needed for that conclusion, that God Himself must have told it to us, and that we do believe His Word by faith; that is to say, by that disposition which is supernaturally given unto us, to believe what God has said, to yield to His Word. God does reveal such unto me, and he does so by His Church; at once I leap forth from myself, I dart upwards unto Him, and I accept as Truth, that which He deigns to reveal thus unto me. And we confess our God thus: *Credo in unum Deum Patrem Omnipotentem.*

Factorem coeli et terrae visibilium omnium et invisibilium. God made Heaven and earth, all things visible and invisible. The Gnostics were loath to attribute to God the creation of matter and of visible beings; this decision of the Council of Nicaea condemns them, formulating with precision, that all things visible and invisible, *visibilium et invisibilium,* were the work of God. Homage is hereby paid to the God Eternal, as being the Almighty, and as having, by this His Omnipotence, created all things visible and invisible. Hereby also is made a profession of faith in the creation of the angels.

Et in unum Dominum, Jesum Christum, Filium Dei Unigenitum. Here again Holy Church would have us say: I believe in *one* Lord. This word *unum* is essential; it is not in two Sons that we believe, but One Alone; it is not in a man and in a God, both separate, and forming two different persons; no, it is the one same Person, that of the only Son of God. But why is He here called Lord in so marked a manner? We did not do so, when we were just now speaking of the Father. This title is specially given to Jesus Christ, because we belong to Him, twice over. We are, first of all, His, because we were created by Him, together with the Father, who hath made all things by His Word; again, we are His, because He redeemed us by His Blood and snatched us from the jaws of Satan; we are His own purchase, His property, His possession; so that He holds us as His by a second right and title, over and beyond that of Creator; and, what is more, His love for souls goes to such a length, as to possess them in title of spouse. That there should be a Son, in the Godhead, verily our knowing this is a sample of a knowledge of God differing far from that mere rational knowledge, of which we were just now speaking. Left to herself, reason could never have taught us that in God there is a Father and a Son; to come to this knowledge, we should need either to have been in Heaven, or to have had this truth revealed to us in Scripture or by Tradition. In the same way, as we believe in one only God the Father, and not in two, so do we believe in one only Son; *et in unum Dominum Jesum Christum, Filium Dei unigenitum.*

Et ex Patre natum, ante omnia saecula: born of the Father before all ages. Ages began only when God sent forth Creation from His hands; that ages might be, time must needs exist, and that time might be, created beings were necessary. Now, before all ages, before aught had yet stepped forth from nothingness, the Son of God had issued from the Father, as we here confess in these words: *Ex Patre natum ante omnia saecula. Deum de Deo, lumen de lumine, Deum verum de Deo vero.* The created world proceeds from God, because it is His handiwork; but for all that, it is not God. The Son of God, on the contrary, coming from the Father, is God as He is, because Begotten by Him: in so much, that all that is said of the Father befits the Son, save only that He is not the Father; but He is ever the same Substance, the same Divine Essence. But still, how can the Son be the same Substance as the Father, without this Substance becoming thereby exhausted? Saint Athanasius, speaking on this subject, gives us the following comparison, which, although material, enables us, in some measure, to seize this Truth. In the same manner, says he, as a torch lighted from another of the same substance, in no way lessens that from which it is lighted, so also the Son of God, taking the Substance of the Father, in no way diminishes this Divine Substance which He shares with Him; for He is in very deed, *God of God, Light of Light, True God of True God.*

Genitum non factum: begotten not made. We human creatures have all of us been made, we are the work of God, every one of us, not even excepting our Blessed Lady and the angels. But as to the Word, the Son of God, it is not so: He is Begotten, not made; He came forth from the Father, but He is not His work. He has the same

Substance, the same Essence, the same Nature as the Father. In God, it behoves us ever to make distinction of Persons, but we must also ever behold the same Divine Substance, as well for the Father and the Son, as for the Holy Ghost: *idem quoad substantiam*. Our Lord also tells us so Himself: *Ego et Pater unum sumus*; they are One, but the Persons are distinct; Father, Son, and Holy Ghost, these are the three terms which serve to designate them. Very important indeed, then, is this great word of the Council of Nicaea: *Consubstantialem Patri*, consubstantial with the Father. Yea, the Son is Begotten by the Father, He has the same Substance; there is the same Divine Essence.

Per quem omnia facta sunt: by whom all things were made. It was said at the beginning of the Symbol, that God made Heaven and earth and all creatures visible and invisible; and now here we are told, speaking of the Word, the Son of God, that all things were made by Him. How are we to reconcile all this? It can easily be understood by means of a comparison with our own soul. Three distinct faculties are given her, for the exercising of these her three distinct acts: power, understanding, and will. These three faculties are necessary to the perfecting of an act. By power, the soul is enabled to act, but this presupposes understanding and will. In like manner God the Almighty Father has made all things by His Power; he has made all things in Wisdom by His Son; and thereon has stamped His Will by the Holy Ghost: and thus is His Act perfected. It is therefore quite correct to say, speaking of the Son: *per quem omnia facta sunt*.

Qui propter nos homines, et propter nostram salutem descendit de coelis. Having shown us the Word operating such great things, Holy Church adds that He has come upon this earth for us sinners. Not only has He come for man's sake, but to repair the sin of man and to snatch him from eternal misery; in a word, to operate our salvation: *et propter nostram salutem*. Yea, on this account is it, that He descended from Heaven: *descendit de coelis*. Nevertheless, He has not quitted the Father and the Holy Ghost, He is not thereby deprived of the Beatitude of the Divinity, but He has truly united Himself to man, and in this Man, He has suffered all that man can suffer, excepting sin; He descended from Heaven, to be in a creature, living in the midst of us, walking with us, conforming Himself in all things to the exigences of human nature.

Et incarnatus est de Spiritu Sancto. The Word hath become Incarnate, He hath been made flesh, by the operation of the Holy Ghost. All things were made by God, and we have seen how they were made by all the Three Divine Persons. In the Mystery of the Incarnation, likewise, there is the action of these Three Persons. The Father sends His Son, the Son comes down upon the earth, and the Holy Ghost overshadows this sublime Mystery.

Ex Maria Virgine. Note well these words: *ex Maria.* Mary it was who furnished the substance of His Humanity, that substance which was proper and personal thereunto; so that she truly took from Herself to give unto the Son of God, who thereby became indeed Her very Son, how pure must Mary needs have been to have been found worthy to furnish unto the Son of God the substance of His human Being! The Word did not choose to unite Himself to a human creature drawn immediately from nothingness, as was the first man, but He would be of the very race of Adam. In order to effect this, He became Incarnate in the Womb of Mary, which necessitated His being consequently a son of Adam; not only did He descend into Mary, but He took from Mary, *ex Maria*: He is of Her very substance.

Et homo factus est: and He was made Man. The Word of God has not only taken the semblance of man, but He has truly become Man. In these sublime words, we behold the Divinity Itself, espousing the Humanity. A genuflection is here made, as a mark of honour paid to the Mystery of the Incarnation.

Crucifixus etiam pro nobis, sub Pontio Pilato passus et sepultus est. The Apostles' Creed has the same expression; the Apostles were bent on saying that our Lord was crucified, not content with simply stating that He died; and this, because it was of high importance to signalise, to all, the victory of the Cross, over Satan. As we were ruined by the wood, so God willed that our salvation also should be wrought by the wood, as we elsewhere sing: *ipse lignum tunc notavit, damna ligni ut solveret.* Yes; it was fitting that the artifice of our enemy should be foiled by his own trick itself: *et medelam ferret inde, hostis unde laeserat*, and that the remedy should be drawn thence, whence the enemy had taken the poison. It is for this very reason, that the Apostles were careful to lay so much stress on the manner of Christ's being put to death; and when first announcing the faith, to pagans, they at once spoke of the Cross. Saint Paul writing to the Corinthians, tells them that, when he first came amongst them, he had not judged it meet to preach unto them anything else but Jesus, and Jesus crucified: *Et enim judicavi me scire aliquid inter vos, nisi Jesum Christum et hunc crucifixum*. (1 Cor. 2:2). And previously, too, he had said to them: And we preach Christ Crucified: a scandal, indeed, to the Jews, and to the Gentiles foolishness: *Judaeis quidem scandalum, Gentibus autem stultitiam* (1 Cor. 1:23).

Jesus Christ was crucified, and the Creed adds: *pro nobis*. In the same way as we say *propter nos homines descendit de coelis*, it was fitting that Holy Church should impress upon us, that, if our Lord was crucified, it was for us. *Crucifixus etiam pro nobis: sub Pontio Pilato passus*. The name of the Roman governor is here mentioned also by the Apostles, because it marks a date. *Et sepultus est*. Christ suffered; that is very true; but what is just as true also is, that He was buried, and it must needs so have been; for had He not been buried, how could that prophecy have been accomplished, wherein it was said that He should rise again on the third day? By this also was proved the reality of His death, complete and not fictitious death—since burial took place, just as is practised in the case of other men.

Et resurrexit tertia die secundum Scripturas. On the third day, He rose again, as the prophecies had foretold, specially that of the Prophet Jonas. Our Lord Himself had said: this wicked and perverse generation seeketh a sign, but one shall not be given to it, unless it be that of Jonas the Prophet, *nisi signum Jonae prophetae* (Matt. 12:39, Luke 11:29). For just as Jonas was in the whale's belly, three days and three nights, so shall the Son of Man be three days and three nights in the heart of the earth.

Et ascendit in coelum: He ascended into Heaven. The Word of God, coming down on earth to be made man, quitted not His Father's bosom. In this place, it is said that He ascended into Heaven, meaning that His humanity actually went up thither, and that there It was enthroned for eternity.

Sedet ad dexteram Patris. He is seated at the right hand of the Father, as Master and Lord. Indeed, He was always there according to His Divine Nature, but it behoved Him to be there also according to His Human Nature, and this is what is expressed by these words. In fact, this was a necessity, because the Human Nature being united to the Divine Nature in one and the same Person, which is the Person of God the Son, it can in all truth be said: the Lord is seated at the Right Hand of the Father. David foretold this, saying: *Dixit Dominus Domino meo: Sede a dextris meis.* (Ps. 109:1). This is a proof of the intimate union which exists of the Divine Nature with the Human, in the Person of our Lord. For this reason, the Psalm 109 is essentially the Psalm of the Ascension, because that was truly the moment when the Lord, the Father, said to the Lord, the Son: Sit Thou at My right hand: *Sede a dextris meis.*

Et iterum venturus est cum gloria judicare vivos et mortuos. So, as regards our Lord, there is question of two comings: in the first He is born without Glory, and, as Saint Paul expresses it, He annihilates Himself, taking the form of a servant: *Semetipsum exinanivit formam servi accipiens* (Phil. 2:7); whereas in the second, He is to come in glory, *venturus est cum gloria.* And wherefore will He come? Not as, heretofore, to save, but to judge: judicare vivos et mortuos. Not only will He come to judge those who will be still living on earth, at the time of his second coming, but moreover all those dead from the very beginning of the world, because absolutely all must be judged.

Cujus regni non erit finis: and of His kingdom there shall be no end. This refers only to the reign of Jesus Christ in His Sacred humanity, because, in His Divinity He has never ceased to reign. This kingdom of His will not only be glorious, but it will never have an end.

The second part of the Credo here ends, and is the largest portion. It was fitting that in this public confession of our faith, Jesus Christ should be treated of, at greater length, because personally He has done most for us, though He has done nothing without the joint action and concurrence of the other two Divine Persons. Therefore it is, we call Him our Lord: doubtless, this title of Lord befits the Father who created us; but still it is doubly applicable to the Son, who, besides having created us (inasmuch as God hath made all things by His Word), has likewise redeemed us: so that we belong to Him by a double title.

Et in Spiritum Sanctum Dominum et vivificantem. I equally believe in the Holy Ghost, that is to say, by faith I go towards the Holy Ghost, I adhere to the Holy Ghost. And who is the Holy Ghost: *Dominum.* He is the Lord, He is the Master, just as the other two Divine Persons are. But what is He furthermore? *Vivificantem,* He gives life. In the same way as our soul gives life to our body, so does the Holy Ghost give life to our soul. It is this Holy Spirit who animates her by the sanctifying grace, which He pours into her, and thus does He sustain her, make her act, vivify her, and make her grow in love. In like manner also, in the Church, it is the Holy Ghost who maintains all; it is He who makes all these her members, so divers in nation, language, and customs, to live all of the same life, belonging, as they do, to the one same Body, of which Jesus Christ is the Head. In fact, all have the same Faith, all draw the same graces from the same Sacraments, and all are animated by the same hopes, and are in expectation of the realisation of these same; in a word, the Holy Ghost sustains all.

Qui ex Patre Filioque procedit: this same Holy Ghost proceedeth from the Father and the Son. How could one suppose that the Father and the Son are not united? There needs must be a link uniting One to the Other. The Father and the Son are not merely in juxtaposition, but a link unites Them, embraces Them, and this link proceeds from both of Them, forming but One with Them; and this mutual love is no other than the Holy Ghost.

At the Council of Nicaea, in drawing up the Symbol, the main attention of the fathers was directed to what treated of Jesus Christ; at the Council of Constantinople, they resolved upon completing the Nicene Creed, by adding what regards the Holy Ghost, save the words *Filioque*; as they expressed it, the words simply stood *Qui ex*

Patre procedit. The Fathers of this Council saw no necessity of saying more on the subject of the Procession, because the words of our Lord, in the Gospel, leave no doubt on the matter. "I will send you the Spirit of Truth who proceedeth from the Father": *Ego mittam vobis a Patre Spiritum veritatis qui a Patre procedit.* (John 15: 26) He is therefore, likewise the Principle of the Holy Ghost, as He sends Him. The Father sends the Son, and it is evident that the Son emanates from the Father, that He is begotten by Him; our Lord here saying: "I will send you the Spirit", proves that He is Himself the source of the Holy Ghost, as is the Father. And if our Lord adds these words: *Qui a Patre procedit,* He in no way means to say that the Holy Ghost proceeds from the Father only; it is merely in order to give further expression to His own words, and to emphasise that not He alone sends this Divine Spirit, but that the Father, conjointly with the Son, sends Him.

The Greeks refused to admit this Truth, and so raised disputations on this passage, in order to overturn the Dogma of the Trinity. But we believe that the Trinity is linked in Its Three Persons, in this ineffable manner, namely, that the First Person begets the Second; the First and the Second are united to one another by the Third. If belief be refused in this bond produced by the Father and the Son, and linking Them together, the Holy Ghost would be utterly isolated from the Son, the Trinity would be destroyed.

It was in Spain that the addition of the *Filioque* was first of all introduced into the Creed, in order to express with greater precision what the Fathers of Constantinople had declared; this change was begun in the eighth century; but the Roman Church did not adopt it till the eleventh. She knew that such a measure would provoke difficulties; but seeing the necessity, she decided upon it, and since then, this addition to the Symbol has become obligatory on the whole Church.

Qui cum Patre et Filio simul adoratur et conglorificatur. The Holy Ghost must needs be adored, therefore He is truly God. So to be in the True Faith, it suffices not to pay honour only, to the Holy Ghost, He must be adored as God, just as we adore the Father and the

Son, *simul adoratur*: He is adored like the other two Divine Persons, and at the same time as They, *simul*. At these words, Holy Church wishes an inclination of the head to be made, as a homage paid to the Holy Ghost, whose Divinity we are here confessing. *Et conglorificatur*, He is conglorified, that is to say, He receives glory together with the Father and the Son; He is included in the same doxology, or glorification, for doxology means to give glory.

Qui locutus est per prophetas. Here we have another Dogma. The Holy Ghost spoke by the prophets, and the Church proclaims that He did so. In formulating this article she had chiefly in view the confounding of the Marcionites, who taught that there was a Good God and an Evil God; and, according to them, the God of the Jews was not good. The Church here declaring that the Holy Ghost spoke by the Prophets, from the Books of Moses, right up to those which near the time of our Lord—proclaims that the action of the Divine Spirit was spread over our earth, from the very commencement.

On Pentecost Day, He came down upon the Apostles, and descended upon earth, in order to abide there: His mission being wholly different from that of our Lord. The Word made flesh came down to our earth, but after a certain time, He ascended again to Heaven. The Holy Ghost, on the contrary, came, that He might abide with us for ever: so that, our Lord, when announcing the coming Paraclete to His Apostles, said to them: The Father will give you another Paraclete, that he may abide with you for ever (John 14:16). He added, that this Paraclete would teach them all things, by giving them the remembrance of all the things which He Himself had taught them: He will bring all things to your mind, whatsoever I shall have said unto you (John 14:26).

The Church requires to be taught, guided, led, and supported. To whom does it belong to effect all this? Who is it that does it? It is the Holy Ghost, who is to assist her even to the end of the world, according to the promise of our Lord. Thus, the Son has been sent by the Father; and then He ascended into Heaven again: both the Father and the Son sent the Holy Ghost, that He might remain with the Church to the end of the world. Our Lord said: My Father will send you the Spirit: and He also said: I will send you the Spirit: and this, in order to show the relations which exist between the Divine Persons, who can never be isolated one from the other, as the heretics asserted.

Holy Church, then, has put clearly before us the dogma of the Trinity. First of all, we have the Father Almighty, Creator of all things; then, the Son, who came down from Heaven, was made man, and died for us; after which He rose again from death, and ascended triumphantly into Heaven, by His Ascension; finally, we have the Holy Ghost, Lord equally with the Father and the Son, the Giver of Life, who spake by the Prophets, and is God together with the Father and the Son.

After this, follows another subject: *Et unam, sanctam, catholicam et apostolicam Ecclesiam.* Observe, we do not say: I believe in the Church; we simply say, I believe the Church. Why is this? Because the faith which has God for its immediate object, is a movement of our soul towards God; she goes forth towards him, and rests in him; and thus, we believe in God. But, as regards created and intermediate things which concern God, which help us to go to God, but are not God himself—we simply believe them. Thus, for example, we believe the Holy Church, which was founded by our Lord Jesus Christ, and in whose bosom alone is there to be found salvation: I believe the Church: *Credo Ecclesiam.* In this Symbol, which is said in the Mass, this article of our faith is more fully expressed than in the Apostles' Creed, where we are taught to say simply: I believe the holy Catholic Church.

We declare then, first of all, that the Church is one: *Credo unam Ecclesiam.* In the Canticle of Canticles, we have our Lord himself calling her *My one—One is my Dove, my perfect one is but one* (Cant. 6:8). She is, moreover, Holy: *Credo Sanctam Ecclesiam.* We hear the Divine Spouse again saying in the same Canticle: *My Love, my Dove, my Beautiful one...there is not a spot in thee* (Cant. 2:10; 4:7). Writing to the Ephesians, Saint Paul likewise says, that the Church which our Lord presented unto Himself, is a glorious Church, not having spot or wrinkle (Eph. 5); therefore, the Church of Christ is Holy, there are no holy ones, no saints, but within her, and there are always holy ones, saints, within her. Moreover, being holy, she cannot teach aught but the truth. The Church is Catholic: *Credo Ecclesiam Catholicam*; that means, she is universal, because she is spread throughout the whole earth, and because she will continue to exist to the end of time; now both of these are included in the quality of catholicity. Finally, she is apostolic: *Credo Ecclesiam Apostolicam*. Yes, her existence dates from the commencement that is to say, she comes from our Lord Himself; she did not spring up all on a sudden when five, ten, or fifteen centuries had gone by, as was the case with Protestantism, for example; had she come thus tardily into being, she could not have come from our Lord. In order to her being the true Church, she must be apostolic, that is, she must have a hierarchy which dates back even to the Apostles, and, by the Apostles, to our Lord Himself.

Thus, we believe the Church; and God wishes us to believe her to be One, Holy, Catholic, and Apostolic: *Et Unam, Sanctam, Catholicam, et Apostolicam Ecclesiam*. We believe her, because she is founded upon these four essential Marks, which are the very meaning of her being called a Church of divine institution, and she is proved to be that, by the very fact of her having those four Marks.

Confiteor unam baptisma in remissionem peccatorum: I confess one Baptism for the remission of sins. The word *Confiteor* signifies here I acknowledge. But why does Holy Church oblige us to confess so expressly one only Baptism: *Confiteor unum baptisma?* Because she is bent on proclaiming that there is but one mode of spiritual birth, and, according to the words of the Apostle to the Ephesians, that there is but one only Baptism, as there is but one only God, and one only Faith: *Unus Dominus, una fides, unum baptisma* (Eph. 4:5).

Baptism makes us become children of God, at the same time giving us sanctifying grace, by which the Holy Ghost comes to dwell within us. And when, by mortal sin, man has the misfortune to lose this grace, Absolution, reconciling him to God, gives back to him this grace of Baptism, this primordial sanctification, and not another; so strong is this first grace. Baptism derives all its power from the water which flowed from our Lord's side, and which hence became for us the very principle of life; therefore our Lord did truly bring us forth; and this is the one only Baptism which we must confess and acknowledge.

Et exspecto resurrectionem mortuorum: I expect the resurrection of the dead. The Church does not tell us to say merely: I *believe* the resurrection of the dead, but I *expect*. We ought, indeed, to be impatient to see the coming of that moment of the resurrection, for the union of the body with the soul is necessary to the perfection of beatitude. The pagans had great difficulty in accepting this Truth, because death seems to be a condition of our very nature; our nature being composed indeed of body and soul, seeing that these elements can be separated, death maintains a certain empire over us. But for us, Christians, the resurrection of the dead is a fundamental dogma. Our Lord Himself, rising again, on the third day after His death, confirms this dogma in a most striking manner; for, says Saint Paul, He is the first to come forth from amongst the dead: *primogenitus ex mortuis*; as we are all to imitate Him, we too must all rise again.

Et vitam venturi saeculi. I expect, likewise, the life of the world to come, which knoweth not death. On earth, we live by the life of grace, we are supported by Faith, Hope, and Charity; but we do not see God. In glory, on the contrary, we shall fully enjoy the sight of Him, we shall see Him face-to-face, as Saint Paul tells us: *Videmus nunc per speculum in enigmate, tunc autem facie ad faciem* (1 Cor. 13:12). Moreover, during the days of our earthly pilgrimage, we are exposed to the danger of losing grace; whereas, in Heaven, no further fear of this kind can exist any longer, and we are put in possession there, of that which alone can fully satiate the boundless cravings of the heart of man; we are put in possession of God Himself, who alone is the end of man. With good reason, then, does Holy Church bid us say: *Et exspecto vitam venturi saeculi.*

Such is the magnificent confession of Faith, put by Holy Church into the mouth of her children. There is yet another formula of our Creed, which was composed by Pius IV, after the Council of Trent. This, which we have just been explaining, is included in it, but with several other articles directed against Protestants, who, when they wish to make their abjuration, are required to read it aloud; without this condition being fulfilled, they could not receive absolution. In like manner, all holders of benefices, before taking possession thereof most pronounce this formula of Faith; for this reason, a bishop does so, on arriving in his diocese.

THE OFFERTORY

When the Symbol of Faith has been chanted by the faithful, the priest kisses the altar, and turning towards the people, he says: *Dominus vobiscum*, to which the usual response is given: *Et cum Spiritu tuo.* Wherefore does the priest kiss the altar? Because being on the point of turning to the faithful, he wishes to salute them with the kiss of Christ, and Christ Himself is represented by the altar.

Next comes the reading of the Offertory: this is a modern custom, because formerly whatever was sung by the choir was never said at the altar. The distinctive functions of the different clerical orders are very clearly marked at this portion of the Mass: to the deacon it belongs to present the paten with the host upon it, to the priest. The deacon cannot consecrate, but he may carry the Holy Eucharist, he may even touch and administer It; so we are not astonished to see what he is now doing; whereas we see the subdeacon remaining much further off from the celebrant.

The priest, on receiving the paten and whilst offering the host, says the prayer: *Suscipe, sancte Pater.* This prayer dates from the eighth or ninth century.

In order the better to understand all these prayers which now follow, we must keep steadily before us the Sacrifice itself, although it is not as yet offered in all its august reality. As a first instance, we have in this prayer, the host spoken of as being presented to the Eternal Father, although our host at this moment is not yet the Divine Host Itself. And it is said that this host is without spot: *immaculatam hostiam*; in these words allusion is made to the victims of the Old Testament, which were obliged to be without blemish, because they were a type of our Lord, who was one day to appear before us as the *Immaculatus*.

In this prayer the thought of the priest runs far on, from the present moment; he is thinking of the host which will be on the altar after Consecration, the host which alone is the True Victim. And for whom does he offer it? Here we see the advantage of our being actually present and assisting at the Mass; for not only does the priest offer it for himself but also for those who are surrounding him: *pro omnibus circumstantibus*. He continually keeps mentioning all those who are here present. But more than this; the action of the Holy Sacrifice of the Mass extends so far, that the priest speaks also of all the faithful, and takes care not to omit the dead; of these last, he presently makes mention saying: *pro omnibus fidelibus Christianis vivis atque defunctis*; for not only is the Sacrifice intended to give glory unto God, but it is meant likewise to procure good things for man.

The four prayers of the Offertory are not very ancient; it was formerly left to the option of the different churches, to choose their own formula of prayer for this moment; the Canon alone has undergone no local changes; it has always been the very same everywhere. Since Pope Pius V issued his missal, which is the one now in use, nothing may be altered in any of the formulae accepted therein by him; but the variety of epoch from which the several prayers date, explains the vast difference observable in the Latin of their composition and in that of the Canon, which is far more beautiful.

The priest having finished the oblation prayer, makes the Sign of the Cross with the paten and places the host on the corporal. This form of the cross expresses the identity existing between the Sacrifice of the Mass and that of Calvary. Next, the deacon puts wine into the chalice, and the subdeacon approaches to fulfil his office, which consists in putting the water into this same chalice; this act is the highest of all his functions.

The prayer which accompanies this ceremony is very ancient; it dates back as far as the first ages of the Church, and indeed it is easy to see that the Latin was a spoken language at the time it was composed. In it is strongly brought before us what is the importance, what the dignity of the water here used in the Holy Sacrifice. Why is water put in the Chalice? Because, according to Tradition, our Lord Himself when instituting the Holy Eucharist, mixed water with the wine, as the abstemious are wont to do, and the Church continues to observe this custom. She avails herself of this opportunity to speak to us in wonderful language, unfolding to us sublimest mysteries.

Thus says Mother Church: *Deus, qui humanae substantiae dignitatem mirabililer condidisti.* Why speak here of the dignity of man? Why recall here, the Divinity and Humanity of Jesus Christ? Because the wine and water here used are figures: the wine represents Jesus Christ as God, the water represents Him as Man. The weakness of the water, compared with the strength of the wine, expresses the difference which exists between the Humanity and the Divinity of Jesus Christ. We must see ourselves too in this water, since we it was, who by Mary, furnished our Lord with the Humanity; thus does Holy Church express herself on this subject, in sentiments of admiration; thus does she love to put forward the true dignity of man.

Already had the royal prophet sung this our dignity, in his Psalm: *Constituisti eum super opera manuum tuarum, omnia subjecisti sub pedibus ejus*: Lord, Thou hast placed man over all the Works of Thy Hands; Thou hast put all things under his feet (Ps. 8). And if we recollect the manner of his creation by God, we are not surprised to hear Holy Church here saying that he was created *in an admirable manner.* When there is question of man, God speaks this word: "Let Us make man to Our Own Image and Likeness." And as He said, so hath He done.

But if man has been thus created, he has been moreover, *raised up in a still more admirable manner,* after his fall, and Holy Church fails not to say so: *mirabilius reformasti.* Yes indeed, God has upraised him in a manner far exceeding, in wonder, that of His Creation, in espousing human nature by His Son, and so reforming fallen man.

Da nobis per hujus aquae et vini mysterium, ejus divinitatis esse consortes, qui humanitatis nostrae fieri dignatus est particeps, Jesus Christus Filius tuus Dominus noster. Make us, by the mystery of this water and of this wine, participators of the Divinity of Him, who hath deigned to make Himself participator of our humanity, Jesus Christ Thy Son, our Lord. Holy Church here puts before us, first of all, in bold relief, the Mystery of the Incarnation, by means of this thought of the water and the wine being mingled together in one potion; thus does she recall the union of the Humanity and the Divinity of our Lord, and she asks of God that we too may participate in the Divinity of the Lord Himself, just as Saint Peter expresses it, in his second Epistle: *ut per haec efficiamini divinae consortes naturae,* that is to say, that by the promises which were fulfilled in Jesus Christ, *we may be made participators of the Divine Nature.* This deification, begun on earth by sanctifying grace, will be completed in Heaven in glory. In the terrestrial paradise, the devil told Eve that if she and Adam would only follow his counsel, both of them should be as gods. Herein he lied; for then, as now, by the faithful fulfilment of the divine precepts alone, can man ever attain unto God. In Heaven, we shall be as gods, not that we shall become so, by nature, but that in the Beatific Vision, we shall see God even as He sees Himself, and our state will be that of creatures placed immediately below the Divinity. Holy Church is bent on holding this Truth before our mental gaze, and she does so in this Prayer, while speaking to us of the Incarnation of the Word, the very principle of man's true greatness.

In Masses of the Dead, the priest does not bless the water, and here we are touching a second mystery. As we have said, the water represents the faithful, and the wine, our Lord Jesus Christ. The use of water and wine is then the figure of two mysteries at once: the mystery of the union of the human with the Divine Nature in our Lord; then, the union of Jesus Christ with His Church, which is composed of all the faithful. Now, the Church has no jurisdiction over the souls in Purgatory; she can no longer exercise over them the Power of the Keys. So long as her children are on earth, she makes use, in their regard, of the Power given her, by our Lord, of binding and loosing; and thus does she lead each soul, either to the Church Triumphant—and then the Church on earth bows down in honour before that happy soul—or, to the Church Suffering, and then the Church on earth prays for that poor soul. But as to exercising any jurisdiction whatsoever, over that soul, she can do so no longer; intercession is all she now has to offer. This is what Holy Church expresses, by omitting the blessing of the water, in Masses of the Dead; she thereby shows that she can exercise no authority over the souls in Purgatory.

Water is so indispensable for the Holy Sacrifice of the Mass, that if it should happen that none could be procured, it would be necessary to abstain from saying Mass, even were it Easter Day.

On the other hand, water may never be mingled in so large a proportion as to alter the wine itself; for in such case, consecration would not take place.

The Carthusians who follow the Liturgy of the eleventh century, and the Dominicans who follow that of the thirteenth, do not perform this ceremony in the Church; they do so in the sacristy, and sometimes at the altar, but always before commencing the Mass.

The water and wine being mingled in the chalice, the priest offers this chalice to God saying these words: *Offerimus tibi, Domine, Calicem salutaris, tuam deprecantes clementiam, ut in conspectu Divinae majestatis tuae, pro nostra et totius mundi salute, cum odore suavitatis ascendat. Amen.* We offer to Thee, O Lord, the Chalice of Salvation, invoking Thy clemency, that it may ascend as an odour of sweet fragrance, before Thy Divine Majesty, for our salvation and that of the whole world. Amen.

In this prayer, Holy Church is thinking, in advance, of that which this chalice is to be come. As yet it holds only wine; but, later on, there will remain of this wine only the accidents, the species or appearances; the substance will give place to the very Blood of our Lord Himself. Holy Church, therefore, prays God to vouchsafe to look beyond that which she is actually offering to Him at this moment—and she begs that this chalice may be in His sight as an odour of sweetness, that is to say, that it may be agreeable to His Divine Majesty, so as to operate the salvation of us all.

The prayer of the Offertory being ended, the priest places the chalice on the corporal, making the Sign of the Cross with the paten, first of all, on the spot whereon it is to stand, in order, thereby, to show, yet once again, that this Sacrifice is truly that of the Cross. In the Latin Church, the bread is placed on the altar in front of the priest, the chalice between the bread and the altar cross: thus, the two offerings are in a line, one in front of the other. The Greeks, on the contrary, place them one beside the other, in a parallel line, the host to the left, the chalice to the right. The chalice once placed on the corporal is again covered with the pall. The pall is a linen cloth, stiffened so as to give it a certain degree of consistence, and which is placed on the chalice to prevent anything falling into it, specially after consecration. Formerly, the pall was not used, the corporal being then large enough to be drawn up over the chalice. This custom is still observed by the Carthusians. Convenience and economy led to the adoption of the pall; but in order to show that it is really no other than a part of the corporal itself, the pall is treated with the very same degree of dignity. The blessing which it receives puts it in a rank apart from such common things as may be handled by anyone; and what shows further that it is one and the same with the corporal, is that the same form of blessing is used for both. At Rome, the pall is made of two pieces of linen sewn together and starched. In our countries it is more usual to put thin cardboard between the two pieces of linen.

Another prayer follows the offering of the chalice, which is recited by the priest at the middle of the altar, having his hands joined and his head somewhat inclined: *In spiritu humilitatis et in animo contrito suscipiamur a te, Domine, et sic fiat hoc sacrificium in conspectu tuo hodie ut placeat tibi, Domine Deus.* In a spirit of humility and in contrite heart, we beg of Thee, O Lord, that we may be received by Thee, and that our Sacrifice may be such, this day in Thy sight, that it may be acceptable to Thee, O Lord, our God. This is a general prayer placed here by Holy Church to complete the Sacred Rites. The words are those of the Three Children in the Fiery Furnace, as related in the Book of Daniel (3:39–40).

Next follows a very important benediction; the Holy Ghost must needs be invoked that He may deign to come down and operate in the Holy Sacrifice; the priest does so in these words: *Veni, Sanctifica-tor, Omnipotens aeterne Deus, et benedic* (saying this word, he makes the Sign of the Cross on all the things offered) *hoc sacrificium in tuo nomini praeparatum.*

As it is the Holy Ghost Himself who operates the change of the bread and wine into the Body and Blood of our Lord, in the Holy Sacrifice of the Mass, it is right that this Divine Spirit should be mentioned in the course of the Sacrifice. Holy Church here invokes Him by this prayer, in order that as He produced our Lord Jesus Christ in the womb of Mary, so He would deign to produce Him again here upon our altar. She expresses this her request in the form of craving a blessing: Bless, says she, this Sacrifice, that is to say, make it fruitful, so that it may be pleasing to the Divine Majesty.

INCENSING OF THE ALTAR, ETC.

We have already seen how the altar represents our Lord; this explains why it is treated with so much honour; the rest of the Church represents the members of the Mystical Body of which Christ is the Head, that is to say, the faithful of whose aggregate Holy Church, the Bride of Christ, is composed. On first going up to the altar, the priest has already incensed it in every direction, thus paying homage to Christ Himself. Now again, this ceremony is performed with sacred pageantry; just as the Eastern Kings laid their rich gifts at the feet of the Divine Infant, as the Gospel tells us, so too is the priest about to burn incense, in his turn, as a homage to his Master and his King.

But, another ceremony must precede that of the incensing of the altar itself. This bread and wine just offered by the priest have been raised above the order of common things by this very offering made of them, so much so indeed, that were the priest to die at this moment of the function, this bread and wine must be disposed of in the piscina. To show her reverence for them, Holy Church sheds on them the perfume of her incense, as if she were doing so to Christ

himself. This custom of using perfumes in Church ceremonies began in the East, where they can be procured in rich abundance. But
in our cold countries though it is much more difficult to get them,
Holy Church will not allow our ceremonies to be utterly deprived
of them, and so she prescribes the use at least of incense, just as for
the Chrism, she will at least have balsam mixed with the oil. After
the incensing of the bread and wine, *incensatio super oblata*, the altar
itself is honoured in like manner. Before making use of the incense,
it must be blessed; the priest does so by the following prayer: *Per in-
tercessionem beati Michaelis Archangeli stantis a dextris altaris incensi....*
The angel who holds the golden thurible in the Apocalypse is not
named. Holy Church here names Saint Michael, Prince of the Heavenly hosts. Some have thought that there is an error in this passage,
because in Saint Luke, the Angel Gabriel is named standing at the
right of the altar; but Holy Church pays no heed to these their ob-
jections; Saint Luke does not say that Gabriel held a golden thurible.
The first blessing of the incense was less solemn; the priest then
only said: *Ab illo benedicaris in cujus honore cremaberis.* Mayst thou be
blessed by Him in honour of whom thou art to be burned. But in
this place, the angels are called upon because the mystery of incense
is no other than the prayer of the saints presented to God, by the
angels, as Saint John tells us, in His Apocalypse (8:4): The smoke
of the incense ascends as does the prayer of the saints before the
Throne of God: *Et ascendit fumus incensorum de orationibus sanctorum
de manu Angeli coram Deo.*

The priest incenses the bread and wine in such a way, that its
odour may perfume, and wholly cloud in fragrance the things offered; while so doing, he says these words: *Incensum istud a te ben-
edictum, ascendat ad Te Domine, et descendat super nos misericordia tua.*
May this incense, O blessed by Thee, ascend to Thee, O Lord, and
may Thy Mercy descend upon us. This prayer, whilst being a homage paid to God, is a wish expressed for ourselves also. The priest
divides these words, at intervals, whilst incensing at several parts
to be thus honoured, in performing which ceremony, he follows
what the rubrics prescribe. When he first incensed the altar, the

priest said no prayer; but now, when thus honouring it a second time, Holy Church bids him repeat a portion of Psalm 140, which she selects, chiefly on account of these words which occur therein, and which are the first she puts on the lips of the priest: *Dirigatur, Domine, oratio mea sicut incensum in conspectu tuo.* May my prayer, O Lord, ascend as incense in Thy sight. It is thus she always does, ever selecting with wonderful appropriateness whatsoever suits the circumstance, whether in Psalms, or in Gospels and Epistles. The priest begins by incensing the Cross, or the Most Holy Sacrament if exposed; he then bows before the Cross, or genuflects, if the Most Holy Sacrament is reserved in the Tabernacle of that altar; then, if there be relics there exposed, he incenses them with two throws of the thurible, first on the Gospel side, then on the Epistle side; after which he incenses every part of the altar. In all other respects, this incensing differs in no way from the first, nor from that which is performed at Lauds and Vespers.

On returning the thurible to the deacon, the priest gives expression to a good wish in his regard as well as in his own, saying: *Accendat in nobis Dominus ignem sui amoris et flammam aeternae charitatis.* May the Lord enkindle in its the fire of His Love and the flame of everlasting charity. On taking the thurible, the deacon kisses the priest's hand, and then the top of the chains; he does the contrary, on presenting it. These customs have come to us from the East, and, inasmuch as they are marks of reverence and respect, it is to the liturgy we owe the preservation of them. The deacon then honours the priest with incense, who receives it standing sideways to the altar; but if the Most Holy Sacrament be exposed, as, for instance, at the Mass of Reposition, the priest comes down from the altar, and with his face turned to the people, he receives the said honours from the deacon, who likewise suits his position to the occasion. Then follows the incensing of the choir, beginning with the bishop, if present; next the prelates, if there then the priests and clerics; and, finally, all the faithful, to show that all form but one Body, of whom Jesus Christ is the Head. All, whether bishops, prelates, or simple faithful, should rise on receiving the incense; the pope alone remains seated for its reception.

LAVABO, PSALM 35

Whilst the choir and people are being honoured with incense, the priest washes his hands. This ceremony is marked, at this particular moment, because the priest has just been using the thurible, which always soils the hands, because of the smoke. But at the same time, this washing of the hands embodies a mystery: it expresses the necessity there is for the priest to purify himself yet more and more, as he advances in the Holy Sacrifice. Just as our Lord washed the feet of His Apostles before instituting the Holy Eucharist and giving them Holy Communion, so too, should the priest purify himself. In the Ambrosian liturgy, this rite of washing the hands takes place during the Canon, before the Consecration; the signification is ever the same, namely, the duty of self-purification incumbent on the priest; nevertheless, the moment chosen for this rite by the Roman Church, ever discreet in all her decisions, is preferable to that adopted by the Ambrosian liturgy.

To accompany this action, which signifies what the purity of the priest should be, Holy Church has selected the Psalm 25, which is marked in the monastic office in the first nocturn of Sunday's Matins: *Judica me, Domine, quoniam ego in innocentia mea ingressus sum.* In this Psalm, it is our Lord Himself who speaks; it is easy to perceive that the priest could never apply such words to himself. Holy Church appoints but the half of this Psalm to be said, commencing with the words: *Lavabo inter innocentes manus meas et circumdabo altare tuum, Domine....* I will wash my hands, O Lord, and make myself like to those who are in the state of innocence, so as to be worthy to approach Thine altar, to hear Thy sacred Canticles and to recount Thy marvellous Works. Every word is wonderfully adapted to the present occasion. Further on, we come across this other remarkable expression of the prophet: *Domine, dilexi decorem domus tuae et locum habitationis gloriae tuae*: Lord, I have loved the beauty of Thy House, the Place where Thy Glory dwelleth. David here speaks of that tabernacle under the shade of which he dwelt so happy, although the temple was not yet in existence, for it was not built till Solomon's time. The Psalm is continued to the end, so as to allow the priest ample time for washing and wiping his hands. This other verse of the same Psalm: *Ego autem in innocentia mea ingressus sum*: I have walked in mine innocence, proves to us, once again, that this Psalm is altogether messianic; the priest, therefore, says it in the Name of Christ, with whom he is but one and the same, during the action of the Great Sacrifice. In Masses of the Dead, and at Passiontide (when the Mass is ferial), the *Gloria Patri* is omitted at the end of this Psalm. This omission of the Gloria in this place is always coupled with the omission of Psalm *Judica* at the beginning of the Mass.

SUSCIPE SANCTA TRINITAS

The priest having ended the Psalm, returns to the middle of the altar, and there, with his hands joined and his head slightly inclined, he says: *Suscipe Sancta Trinitas, hanc oblationem quam tibi offerimus ob memoriam Passionis, Resurrectionis et Ascensionis Jesu Christi Domini nostri....* Things of high import here stand before us. An oblation is spoken of: *Suscipe hanc oblationem*: Receive this oblation. The priest says these words of the bread and wine just offered by him; nevertheless, he has really in view neither this bread nor this wine. These things are, indeed, sanctified and blessed, and hence they deserve to be treated with respect; but the oblation here presented to the Divine Majesty, could never be confined to an order of Sacrifice purely material, as was that of the Jews; it is evident, therefore, that the priest is here stretching forward in thought to a something far higher: he is presenting the offering of the Great Sacrifice which is soon to be accomplished—And, O Holy Trinity, we offer this oblation to Thee, in memory of the Passion, of the Resurrection, and of the Ascension of Jesus Christ, our Lord. So, we must here note these three things in our Lord, without which He would not be complete. First of all, He suffered, but He could not be satisfied with suffering alone, so He died also, and these two coupled, constitute what we call His Passion; but this is not all, the Lord rose again. Death, the punishment of sin, is, as it were, the devil's triumph over man, and therefore it would have been a true defeat suffered by Christ, had He died without afterwards rising again. But further still, He hath gone up into Heaven, by His glorious and triumphant Ascension. Our Lord could not possibly have remained on earth; until He open Heaven, and Himself enter therein, in His Human Nature, Heaven must needs remain closed to man; on this very account, therefore, our salvation is not wholly effected, unless our Lord ascend to Heaven, after having suffered for us, notwithstanding His being truly the Risen-One, being, as Saint Paul expresses it, "the First-Born from amongst the dead!" So, then, let us well drink in this great Truth, namely, that our Lord Suffered, that He Arose, but that man's salvation is not wholly accomplished, if he still abide as an exile on our earth; to the Passion and Resurrection, must needs be added the Ascension. Such, then, should be our Faith, because such is the economy of our Salvation, in which are contained these three things: the Passion, the Resurrection, the Ascension. So well does Holy Church understand that these three are needed to complete Christ, and that therein is our whole Faith comprised, that she makes a point of insisting on our expressing the same in a marked manner, here at this moment of the offering of the Sacrifice.

Et in honorem beatae Mariae semper Virginis. Not a single Mass is offered, but it brings glory to our Blessed Lady, who is, in Herself, a whole world apart. Therefore is it that we first of all recall the memory of our Lord, then of the Blessed Virgin, and finally of the angels and saints. The angels are greater than we, that is to say, they are superior to us, by reason of their spiritual nature; but our Blessed Lady, although a mere human creature, is raised far above them all, because, as before said, she forms a world apart, she is the very masterpiece of God Himself; hence Holy Church fails not to honour her as such in the Holy Sacrifice, wherein she never forgets this sublime queen and the place apart due to her alone.

Et beati Joannis Baptistae. Holy Church holds Saint John the Baptist in great veneration in the *Confiteor*, we have seen, she always mentions him, and here again she is delighted to give fresh honour to

47

the Precursor of our Lord. *Et sanctorum apostolorum Petri et Pauli*; it is right to pay our tribute of glory also to these two great Apostles who laboured together in founding the Holy Roman Church.

Et istorum. This expression has more than once raised a difficulty: it has been asked, many a time, who are hereby intended? Some would have it, that the saint of the day was here referred to; but in such a case, we ought to use the word *istius*, and not *istorum*; and then, again, Masses of the Dead would present another difficulty in the way of such a solution; so it is evident that the Church's meaning must be other than such a supposition. It is plain that she here intends to allude to those saints who are There, that is to say, whose relics are incorporated in the altar itself. For this very reason, when an altar is being consecrated, Relics of several saints must be placed therein; those of one saint only would not suffice and would not justify the Church's expression here: *et istorum*. Yea, says she, in honour of these saints who here serve as the resting place of the mystery which is established upon them, of these saints on whose bodies the Great Sacrifice is to be accomplished: what could be more fitting than to make special mention apart of these saints

Et omnium sanctorum.... Finally, Holy Church mentions all the saints, in general, because all have part in the Holy Mass. *Ut illis proficiat ad honorem, nobis autem ad Salutem....* Observe here two things coupled in the Holy Sacrifice: on the one hand, it gives glory to God, to the Blessed Virgin Mary, and to the saints; on the other, it is profitable to us; the Church, therefore, makes us here beg of God to deign to accept it so, that it may attain this double end proposed. As to the words which terminate this prayer, they give us a form of invoking the saints whom Holy Church specially commemorates on that particular day: *Et illi pro nobis intercedere digneris in coelis quibus memoriam agimus in terris. Per eumdem Christum Dominum nostrum*; note how the name of Christ is always added.

This prayer, like the first, has only been fixed for universal use, since the time of Saint Pius V. Its Latin is less fine than that of the Canon, which originates from the earliest Christian ages, as does also the prayer for the benediction of the water, which we have given above.

ORATE FRATRES

Then the priest, having kissed the altar, turns towards the people with this salutation: *Orate, fratres, ut meum ac vestrum sacrificium acceptabile fiat apud Deum Patrem Omnipotentem.* These words form the priest's farewell to them, for he will not again turn to them, until the Sacrifice is consummated. But, observe that this is not his ordinary parting word; as, for instance, when he went up to the altar, his merely said *Dominus vobiscum*. In this place, he recommends himself to the prayers of the faithful, in order that this Sacrifice, which belongs, at once, both to priest and people, may be pleasing unto God. The Sacrifice is the priest's, for he is the direct agent therein; the Sacrifice belongs to the faithful, because Jesus Christ instituted it for their particular profit; see now why it is that the priest lays such stress upon these words: *meum ac vestrum sacrificium*. For the very same reason, likewise, he re-awakens the attention of the faithful, urging them more and more to earnestness; for it behoves them not to forget, that they too have a share in the priesthood, as says Saint Peter, calling the faithful a kingly priesthood, *regale sacerdotium* (1 Pet. 2:9), by the mere fact that they are Christians. They come from Christ, they belong to Christ, they have been anointed, and by their very baptism have become *other Christs*; needs must be, therefore, that they too hold the power of offering Sacrifice in union with the priest. Thus, aroused by the priest's voice, they hasten to respond to his desire, by giving expression to their own hearty wish: *Suscipiat Dominus sacrificium de manibus tuis, ad laudem et gloriam nominis sui, ad utilitatem quoque nostram, totiusque Ecclesiae suae sanctae.* May the Lord receive this Sacrifice from thy hands, for the praise and glory of His name, for our own weal, and for that of His Holy Church. The missal still retains in a parenthesis, in this place, the word *meis* to suit an occasion in which the priest himself might be obliged to supply for the absence or ignorance of the server of his Mass.

This response having been made by the faithful, they should reflect how they will indeed see the priest's face no more, until the Lord Himself has come down on our altar. His voice even will not be heard again, save once; and that will be for the intoning of the great and magnificent prayer of thanksgiving, namely, the Preface.

But, before this, he collects the desires of the faithful, into one prayer, which, as he says it in an undertone, has received the name of the *secret*; for the same reason that he prays here in silence, he does not precede it with the usual word *Oremus*, Let us pray, inasmuch as he is not now convening the faithful to make it with him. In the sacramentaries, that of Saint Gregory, for example, this prayer is entitled: *Oratio super oblata*.

PREFACE

Although the priest has been making his petitions in a low voice, yet he terminates this his prayer aloud, exclaiming: *Per omnia saecula saeculorum*; to which the faithful respond *Amen*, that is to say, we ask also, for what thou hast been asking. In fact, the priest never says anything in the Holy Sacrifice without the assent of the faithful, who, as we have already noticed, participate in the priesthood. They have not heard what the priest has been saying, nevertheless they join therein and approve heartily of all, by answering their *Amen*, yea, our prayer is one with thine! The dialogue here begun between priest and people is maintained for a while, at length leaving the final word to the priest alone, who gives thanks solemnly, in the name of all there assembled.

The priest then salutes the people, but this time without turning to them, saying: *Dominus vobiscum*, the Lord be with you: lo! now is the most solemn moment of prayer! And the faithful respond: *Et cum Spiritu tuo*, may He be with thy Spirit, may He aid thee, lo! we are one with thee! Then the priest says: *Sursum Corda!* lift up your hearts! The priest requires that their hearts be detached from earthly thoughts, so that they may be directed on God alone; for the prayer he is about to make is that of thanksgiving. Admire how well placed is this prayer here, for the priest is on the point of accomplishing the Sacrifice of the Body and Blood of our Lord, and this Sacrifice is verily for us the instrument of thanksgiving; it is the means whereby we are enabled to render back to God that which we owe him. So Holy Mother Church, delighting with intensest relish in this magnificent prayer, would fain arouse her faithful children with this cry: *Sursum Corda!* in order that they too may appreciate, as she does, this great act of thanksgiving, whereby she offers unto God a something that is great and worthy of Him. And now the faithful hasten to express their reassurances to the priest: *Habemus ad Dominum!* We have our hearts raised up unto the Lord! Then, replies the priest, if indeed it is so, let us all unitedly give thanks unto the Lord: *Gratias agamus Domino Deo nostro.* And the faithful at once add: *Dignum et justum es!* Thus do they unite themselves wholly with the thanksgiving of the Preface which the priest is about to speak. This dialogue is as old as the Church herself; and there is every reason to believe that the Apostles themselves arranged it, because it is to be found in the most ancient Churches and in all liturgies. As far as possible, the faithful should make an effort never to be seated on any account during these acclamations. Now does the priest take up the speech himself and continues thus alone: *Vere dignum et justum est, aequum et salutare, nos tibi semper et ubique, gratias agere: Domine Sancte, Pater omnipotens, aeterne Deus, per Christum Dominum nostrum.* So it is truly just to give Thee thanks, O Almighty God, *tibi* to Thee, Thyself, *semper et ubique*, always and everywhere, and to render Thee this our thanks, through Jesus Christ, our Lord. Yes, indeed, it is through Jesus Christ that our thanksgiving must be made, for were we to do so in our own name, there would be the infinite between God and ourselves, and so our thanksgiving could never reach unto Him; whereas, made through Jesus Christ, it goes straight up, and penetrates even right to the very centre of the Divinity. But, not only must we, human creatures, go to the Father through our Lord, but the very angels even, have no access except through Him. Hearken once more to the priest: *Per quem Majestatem tuam laudant angeli*, by whom (i.e., Jesus Christ), the angels praise Thy Majesty for, since the Incarnation, they adore the Godhead, through Jesus Christ, our Lord, the Sovereign High Priest. *Adorant Dominationes*, the Dominations adore through Jesus

Christ; *tremunt Potestates*, the Powers too, those beauteous angels, make their celestial thrillings heard, and in awe, tremble before the Face of Jesus Christ: *Coeli*, the Heavens, that is to say, angels of still higher order; *coelorumque Virtutes*, and the Heavenly Virtues also, angels yet more exalted; *ac beata seraphim*, and the Blessed Seraphim, who by their pure love come nighest unto God—*socia exsultatione concelebrant*, all these stupendous choirs blended together in one harmonious transport concelebrate, through Jesus Christ, the Majesty Divine. The Prefaces thus terminate by mentioning the angels, in order to lead the Church Militant to sing the hymn of the Church triumphant. *Cum quibus et nostras voces ut dimitti jubeas deprecamur, supplici confessione dicentes*; yea, fain are we to join anon our feeble voice to that mighty angelic strain, and we crave leave to begin even now whilst here below, and sinners still, the great: *Sanctus, Sanctus, Sanctus, Dominus Deus Sabaoth*.

Thus all Prefaces are formed on the one great idea of giving thanks to God, *gratias agere*; and of making this thanksgiving *through Jesus Christ*, because it is by Him alone that we can come nigh unto God, yea, approach in union with the angels too, with whom we join in the celestial chorus of their Trisagion.

Besides this the Common Preface, Holy Church offers us others wherein we invite the Heavenly Spirits to celebrate with us, in one joint act of thanksgiving, the principal Mysteries of the Man-God, whether at Christmas or in Lent, or at Passiontide, or at Easter, or, again, at Ascension or Pentecost. Nor does she fail to remember her by whom Salvation came to this our earth, the Glorious Virgin Mary; as also the Holy Apostles by whom redemption was preached to the entire world.

The Preface is intoned on the very same melody used by the ancient Greeks when celebrating some hero in their feasts, and there declaiming his mighty deeds in song.

SANCTUS

The Trisagion is the hymn heard by Isaias when favoured with a vision of Heaven, and later by Saint John also, as he relates in his Apocalypse (4: 8). The Church could not well have placed this song of Heaven at the beginning of the Mass, whilst we were just confessing ourselves sinners before God and the whole celestial court. What, then, is it the angels say? *Sanctus, Sanctus, Sanctus, Dominus Deus Sabaoth.* They celebrate the sanctity of God. And how do they celebrate it? In a manner the most complete; they use the superlative, saying thrice over that God is truly holy. We meet with the song Trisagion in the *Te Deum* also: *Tibi Cherubim et Seraphim incessabili voce proclamant: Sanctus, Sanctus, Sanctus, Dominus Deus Sabaoth.*

Wherefore is it that God is thus expressed by the triple affirmation of holiness? Because holiness is the chief perfection of God: God is Holy by Essence.

In the Old Testament even, this angelic cry was already made known: the Prophet Isaias heard it; in the New Testament, John, the Beloved Disciple, names it in his Apocalypse. So then, God is indeed holy, He delights in revealing this to us. But, to holiness is added yet more still: *Sanctus Dominus Deus Sabaoth,* holy is the Lord, the God of armies; this is like saying: *Deus Sanctus et fortis,* God, the Holy and the strong. So here we have two things in God, sanctity and strength. This expression *Deus Sabaoth* or *Deus exercituum,* the God of armies, is used, because nothing gives such an idea of strength, as an army surmounting all obstacles, laughing at difficulties, and overriding all that comes in its way: thus is the strength of God vividly expressed. So then, God is holy and strong. This angelic song has received the name of the Trisagion, which is derived from *Agios,* holy, and from *tris,* three: God, the thrice holy.

In the Old Testament a notion of the Holy Trinity was hereby conveyed, as though it stood thus: holy is God the Father, holy is God the Son, holy is God the Holy Ghost. But in order to catch a glimpse of this truth, it was needful to be learned in the understanding of the Scriptures; hence, hardly any but the Doctors of the Law could come at this knowledge; or, again, in prayer, God would sometimes vouchsafe to reveal this Truth to privileged souls, in whom He deigned to enkindle his Light. Among the Jews, such favoured souls were always to be found.

After confessing the holiness and strength of God, the Church adds: *Pleni sunt coeli et terra gloria tua*. There is no way, more magnificent than this, of expressing the Glory of God; verily there is no nook or corner of Creation where shines not forth the Glory of God; everything is produced by His Power, and everything gives Him Glory. Holy Church transported on beholding this, cries out aloud: *Hosanna in excelsis*. We read in the Sacred Scriptures that this cry was uttered by the Jews, when Jesus was entering into Jerusalem, on Palm Sunday, and the people shouted *Hosanna filio David*; yes, *Hosanna*, which means Salvation, a salutation of deep respect. Holy Church blends both of these together, making one of the *Sanctus* and of this solemn salutation: *Hosanna in excelsis*, Hosanna in the highest. She could never have let slip such exquisite lore. Just as at the commencement of Mass, she would have us unite with the Angels in chanting the *Kyrie* a very cry of distress, so now she bids us mingle our voices once again with their angelic choirs, but in a manner totally different to the former occasion; lo! now she has entered into the mysteries—she is on the point of coming into complete possession thereof—therefore is she seized with enthusiasm, and her one thought now is to sing to her God: *Sanctus, Sanctus, Sanctus, Hosanna in excelsis*. Verily, the Jews did well to shout their *Hosanna*, as they went, wending in glad procession down the Mount of Olives, towards Jerusalem, entering by the Golden Gate; all was in harmony, and breathed triumph; but how far more fitting is it for us to sing it, at this portentous moment, when the Son of God is about to come down in the midst of us who truly know Him! Well did the Jews shout: *Hosanna*. Hold, still they knew Him not; yet a few days and they would cry against Him: *Tolle, tolle, crucifige eum*.

This Trisagion is to be found in every Church, of whatever liturgy, and whatever rite it may be. Formerly, the *Sanctus* was sung on the Preface tone; and then there was ample time to sing the whole before the Consecration, adding even the words: *Benedictus qui venit in nomine Domini.* Later on, however, it was sung to more elaborate chants; hence arose the somewhat modern custom, of cutting this piece in two, because it was quite possible for the Consecration to take place before its singing was finished. So, the choir now pauses at the *Benedictus*, taking up from there, after the Consecration. Hence this phrase, first intended as a salutation to Him who was about to come, must now be taken in the sense of hailing Him who is come. The priest, however, still recites these words: *Benedictus qui venit in nomine Domini*, immediately after the Trisagion; and in so saying, he makes on himself the sacred sign of our Redemption, to show that these words apply to our Lord Himself. Nevertheless this recitation of the *Sanctus* and the *Benedictus* by the priest must not be considered as comparatively recent, as we said respecting the Introit. For, indeed, we find the *Sanctus* is recited by priests of Oriental rites; now, it is well known that Eastern liturgies have retained their adopted rites from the highest antiquity, without suffering the slightest change therein.

THE CANON OF THE MASS

The Preface being finished, the *Sanctus* is sounded, and the priest then enters within the cloud. His voice will not be heard again, until the great prayer is concluded. This prayer has received the name of *Canon Missae*, that is to say, Rule of the Mass, because it is this portion which essentially constitutes the Mass: it may be well termed the Mass by excellence. It finishes at the *Pater*, and then, as previously at the conclusion of the Offertory prayers, the termination will be signalised by the priest himself, who will utter the concluding words in a loud voice: *Per omnia saecula saeculorum*; to which the faithful will add their *Amen*, we approve of all that has been said and done by thee, because our intention was one and the same with thine, to bring down the Lord into our midst; and therefore are we participators in all thine acts. So then, it is to be observed that the priest says the whole of this great prayer, the Canon, in an undertone, not excepting even the various *Amen* which conclude the separate prayers of which the Canon is composed. Once only, does he raise his voice a little, and then only whilst uttering two or three words, whereby he declares himself to be a sinner, as well as those who are around him: *Nobis quoque peccatoribus.*

In the seventeenth century the Jansenist heretics tried to introduce the abuse of reciting the Canon of the Mass aloud. Deceived by their tricks, Cardinal de Bissy, one of the successors of Bossuet, countenanced the admission of ℟. in red type, into the missal which he had composed for his Church, as the French bishops of that day imagined they had a right to do. These ℟. in red would naturally convey the idea that the people were supposed to respond the *Amen* thus marked. Now they can only respond to prayers that can be heard. Hence would necessarily follow, at last, the recitation of the Canon aloud, by the priest, which was the very thing aimed at by these Jansenists. But happily public attention was quickly drawn to this dangerous innovation, loud complaints were raised against it, and Cardinal de Bissy himself withdrew the unfortunate step he had taken.

The various prayers of which the Canon is composed are of the highest antiquity; nevertheless, they cannot be traced to the very first days of Holy Church; this is proved by the fact that the Divine Service was at first performed in the Greek tongue, a language in much more general use, at that epoch, than the Latin. It is probable, therefore, to suppose that the prayers, such as we have them, were drawn up verging on the second century, or possibly as late as the first years of the third. Every Church has its Canon; but if these differ a little as to form, the substance is always the very same, and the doctrine expressed in their various rites, agrees often identically with that expressed in our Latin rite. We have in this fact, an admirable proof of the unity of belief, be the rite what it may.

The initial letter of the first prayer of the Canon is T, which is equivalent to the Hebrew *Tau* [ת], and which, by its very shape, represents a Cross. No other sign could better be placed as a heading to this great prayer, in the course of which the Sacrifice of Calvary is renewed. Thus it was, that when those magnificent Sacramentaries were first of all written, ornamented with vignettes and rich designs of every kind, this *Tau* was lavishly treated in decoration, and at length came the happy idea of painting a figure of Christ on this Cross, supplied by the text itself. By degrees the design got enlarged, until it ended in becoming a representation of the entire scene of the Crucifixion; still, large as it was, it continued to be merely an adjunct to the initial letter only of the prayer *Te igitur.* But at length, a subject of so great importance, was deemed worthy of being treated quite independently of this, and the result was a separate picture. So that now, there is no complete missal without an engraving of Christ on the Cross, placed on the leaf facing that on which the Canon begins. And this can be traced to the simple fact of this little vignette which ornamented the ancient sacramentaries.

As to the importance of the *Tau* itself, we hear mention of it even in the Old Testament; for Ezechiel says, speaking of the elect, that the blood of the Victim being taken, all those whom God had reserved to Himself should be marked therewith on the forehead with the sign of the *Tau,* and that the Lord had promised to spare all those thus marked (Eze. 9: 46). This is explained by the great fact that we are all saved by the Cross of Jesus Christ, which was made in the form of the *Tau.* In confirmation also the bishop marks the *Tau* with Holy Oil, on the forehead of those whom he confirms. Our Lord's Cross was in the shape of a *Tau,* thus: T. Above it a piece of wood was placed as a support to the title affixed, and thus is completed the shape of the cross such as we now have it; for we learn, in Saint John, that the cause of our Lord's death was placed above the cross: *Scripsit autem et titulum Pilatus, et posuit super crucem* (John 19: 19).

Notice of what high importance is this one letter which commences the great prayer of the Canon.

TE IGITUR

Te igitur, Clementissime Pater, per Jesum Christum Filium tuum Dominum nostrum supplices rogamus ac petimus.

After the *Sanctus*, the priest extends his arms upraised, then joining his hands, he raises his eyes to Heaven, but casts them down again immediately. Then, bowing profoundly, with his hands joined and leaning them upon the altar, he says: *Te igitur, Clementissime Pater.* These words *Te igitur* serve as a link to the one great idea; they express that the priest has but one thought, that of the Sacrifice. It is as though he were saying to God (for all these prayers, as we see from the outset, are addressed to the Father), seeing that I am Thine, seeing that the faithful have now placed all their desires in my hands, behold, we come before Thee, in the name of this very Sacrifice; then he kisses the altar, in order to give more expression to the earnestness of his petition, and continues: *uti accepta habeas et benedicas*, here, he joins his hands and then prepares to begin the Sign of the Cross which he is to make thrice, over the oblation, whilst adding these words, *haec dona, haec munera, haec Sancta sacrificia illibata*; yea, this bread and wine which we have offered to Thee are truly pure; deign then to bless them and receive them; and bless them, not inasmuch as they are mere material bread and wine, but, in consideration of the Body and Blood of Thy Son, into which they are about to be changed. The Sign of the Cross here made by the priest over the bread and wine is especially to show that he has Christ Himself mainly in view.

Again stretching out his hands, he thus continues: *in primis quae tibi offerimus pro Ecclesia tua sancta catholica.* The first interest at stake, when Mass is said, is Holy Church, than which nothing is dearer to God; He cannot fail to be touched, when His Church is spoken of. *Quam pacificare, adunare et regere digneris toto Orbe terrarum.* The word *adunare* gives us here God's own intention regarding her; He wishes her to be one, as He himself says in Holy Writ: *una est Columba mea* (Cant. 6:8). Entering into His Divine views, we too implore of Him to keep her always one, and that nothing may ever succeed in tearing the Seamless Garment of Christ. As in the *Pater* the very first petition that our Lord bids us make, is that This Name may be hallowed: *Sanctificetur nomen tuum*, thereby teaching us that God's Glory and Interests must take precedence of all others; so here, just in the same way, This glory is put forward, in what regards His Church, *in primis*. And our prayer for her is that she may have peace; we ask that she may be protected, that she may be indeed one, and well governed throughout the entire world.

The priest next adds: *una cum famulo tuo Papa nostro N. et Antistite nostro N. et omnibus orthodoxis, atque Catholicae et apostolicae fidei cultoribus*. So, there is not a Mass offered, but it benefits the whole Church; all her members participate therein, and care is taken, in the wording of this prayer, to name them in particular. First of all comes the Vicar of Jesus Christ on earth; and when His name is pronounced, an inclination of the head is made, to honour Jesus Christ, in the person of his Vicar. The only exception to this, is when the Holy See happens to be vacant. When the pope himself is saying Mass, he here substitutes these words: *Et me indigno servo tuo*.... The bishop does in like manner, in his own case, for next after the pope, the missal makes mention of the bishop, in whose diocese the Mass is being celebrated, so that in all places, Holy Church may be represented in her entirety. At Rome, there is no mention made of a bishop, because the pope himself is Bishop of Rome. In order that all her members without exception may be named, Holy Church here speaks of all the faithful, calling them *fidelium*, that is to say, those who are faithful in observing the Faith of Holy Church, for to be included in those mentioned here, it is necessary to be in this Faith; it is necessary to be orthodox, as she takes care to specify, *omnibus orthodoxis*, which means, those who think aright, who profess the Catholic Faith—the Faith handed down by the Apostles. By laying such stress on these words: *omnibus orthodoxis atque catholicae et apostolicae fidei cultoribus*, Holy Church would have us see, that she excludes from her prayer, on this occasion, those who are not of the household of the Faith, who do not think aright, who are not orthodox, who hold not their Faith from the Apostles.

The terms in which Holy Church expresses herself, throughout, show very clearly how far Holy Mass is alien to private devotions. She, then, must take the precedence of all else, and her intentions must be respected. Thus does Holy Church give all her members a participation in the Great Sacrifice; so true is this, that were the Mass to be done away with, we should quickly fall again into the state of depravity in which pagan nations are sunk: and this is to be the work of Antichrist: he will take every possible means to prevent the celebration of the Holy Sacrifice of the Mass, so that this great counterpoise being taken away, God would necessarily put an end to all things, having now no object left in their further subsistence. We may readily understand this, if we observe how, since the introduction of Protestantism, the inner strength of Society has materially waned. Social wars have been waged one after another, carrying desolation along with them, and all this solely, because the intensity of the Great Sacrifice of the Mass has been diminished. Terrible as this is, it is but the beginning of that which is to happen, when the devil and his agents let loose upon the earth, will pour out a torrent of trouble and desolation everywhere, as Daniel has predicted. By dint of preventing ordinations, and putting priests to death, the devil will at length prevail so far as that the celebration of the Great Sacrifice will be suspended—then will come those days of horror and misery for our earth.

Nor must we be astonished at this, for Holy Mass is an event in God's sight, as well as for us; it is an event which directly touches His Glory. He could not despise the voice of this Blood more eloquent a thousand times, than that of Abel; He is obliged to regard it with special attention, because His own Glory is there at stake, and because it is His own Son Himself, the Eternal Word, Jesus Christ, who is there offering Himself as victim, and who there prays for us to His Father.

In the Holy Eucharist there are three things for us ever to hold in view: firstly, the Sacrifice whereby Glory is given to God; secondly, the Sacrament which is the food of our souls; thirdly, the possession of our Lord personally in His Real Presence, so that we are able there to offer Him that adoration which is the consolation of our exile. This mere possession of our Lord, whereby a means is given us of adoring Him there really present, is the least of these three great things—it is less than the receiving of the Sacrament in Holy Communion; again, if Holy Communion is less than the Sacrifice, because, there, we alone are in question; but when all these Three are unitedly realised, then the whole Mystery is complete, and that which our Lord willed in instituting the Eucharist is brought to pass. Verily, had it been given us but to be permitted to adore the Lord present in our midst, it would indeed have been a wondrously mighty gift, but Holy Communion far surpasses this; and the Sacrifice transcends, beyond all thought, both of these great favours: Lo! by the Sacrifice, we act directly on God Himself, and to that act He cannot be indifferent, else He would thereby derogate from His own Glory. Now, as God has done all things for His Glory's sake, He must needs be attentive to the Holy Sacrifice of the Mass, and must grant, under some form or other, whatsoever is thereby asked of his Divine Majesty. Thus never is one Mass offered without these four great ends of Sacrifice being fulfilled: adoration, thanksgiving, propitiation, and impetration; because God has so pledged himself.

When our Lord was teaching us how to pray, He told us to say: *Sanctificetur nomen tuum*—this is a bold petition, one that very closely touches the interests of God's great Glory—but in Holy Mass, we go further still, we poor creatures may there tell the Mighty God Himself; that He may not turn away from this Sacrifice, for it is even Jesus Christ who is offering it; that He may not refuse to hearken, for it is Jesus Christ Himself who is here praying.

In former times, at this place in the Canon, the name of the king was mentioned after that of the Bishop: *et rege nostro N*...but since Saint Pius V issued his Missal for general use, this has been omitted. Saint Pius V's decision on this point was owing to the difference of religion found amongst princes, since the introduction of Protestantism. Rome alone can give particular permission to name any king in the Canon. Spain petitioned for this favour in the reign of Philip II, and it was granted. In France the Parliament of Toulouse and that of Paris, taking umbrage at the omission of the king's name in the Missal of Saint Pius V. when it first appeared, prohibited the printing of the said missal. In 1855 Napoleon III asked and obtained of the pope authorisation for his name to be mentioned in this part of the Mass.

There is neither the usual form of conclusion, nor the *Amen*, to either the first or second prayer of the Canon.

MEMENTO OF THE LIVING

Memento, Domine, famulorum famularumque tuarum N. et N.... and the priest, joining his hands, recalls in secret, those whom he wishes to recommend to God. Thus has the priest first of all prayed for the whole Church in general, for the pope, the bishop, and all orthodox Catholics, that is to say, all who are of the Faith of Holy Church. But this great Sacrifice, the fruits of which are infinite, operates in a more particular manner on all those, for whom special prayer is made; therefore the priest is allowed here to mention those whom he wishes to recommend to God more especially. We learn from Tradition that in all ages, the priest has been free thus to pray more expressly for those in whom he was interested, because the fruits of the Holy Sacrifice can be applied to them in particular, without prejudice to the principal intention.

Again stretching out his hands, the priest continues his prayer, saying: *Et omnium circumstantium, quorum tibi fides cognita est et nota devotio*.... The priest prays for all those who are present around him, because their faith has urged them to leave alone everything else, and to come gathering about the altar, and for this reason, they deserve a special share in the Holy Sacrifice. See here, how good it is to assist at Mass as often as possible. But if we do so, it must be with faith and devotion, for the priest particularly says: *quorum tibi fides cognita est et nota devotio*. It is quite clear that the priest could never speak thus to God in behalf of such Christians as conduct themselves no differently in Church than they would anywhere else, who are in no way preoccupied with what is going on at the altar, and who seem to have nothing else to do, but to distract themselves as far as they can, more or less respectably. So then of those who are present it is only such as assist with faith and devotion that can participate in the fruits of Holy Mass. As to those who are absent, they too can participate of the Sacrifice, by uniting themselves spiritually thereunto, and by desiring to assist thereat, with faith and devotion, were it in their power to come. If such be their dispositions, they do really share in the fruits of the great Sacrifice, how far soever distant they may be. Observe from all that has been said, how the priest can have no mere personal idea, when approaching the altar to offer Sacrifice. He then holds the whole Church in his hands, and he prays with outstretched arms, like Christ Himself, offering Sacrifice for all men. The priest here adds further instance to his prayer, singling out before God, those divers persons for whom he is offering the Holy Sacrifice: *pro quibus tibi offerimus, vel qui tibi offerunt hoc Sacrificium laudis.* The Church here uses this term Sacrifice of praise (though more properly applied to the Psalmody), because Holy Mass is likewise for the praise and honour of God; besides, this is a Scripture phrase, often to be met with, elsewhere.

For whom is the Sacrifice being offered? The priest, still speaking of those whom he has mentioned, continues his thought, adding: *pro se, suisque omnibus, pro redemptione animarum suarum, pro spe salutis et incolumitatis suae.* Thus does the Holy Sacrifice embrace all, extend to all. The soul holds the first place in this enumeration; and we have here come across that petition, so frequently found in Foundation-Charta of the Middle Ages, namely, *pro redemptione animarum suarum, etc.* The Church next occupies herself with the bodily needs of her children; she begs of God to keep the body safe and sound amidst all the perils by which it is surrounded. Finally, the priest concludes by offering to the living God, the desires and wants of all the faithful, in these words: *tibique reddunt vota sua aeterno Deo vivo et vero.*

The priest cannot here pray either for Jews or for infidels, no more than he can for heretics, who by the very fact of heresy alone, are excommunicates, and consequently out of the pale of the Holy Catholic Church. Neither can he pray for such as, without being heretics, are excommunicated for other causes; it would be a profanation to utter the names of any such in the midst of the Holy Sacrifice. They may be prayed for in private, but not in official prayers. They are excluded from the Sacrifice, as they are out of the Church; consequently, it is impossible to mention them during the Sacred Celebration.

COMMUNICANTES

The Church Militant does not wish to approach the holy altar all alone. She has spoken to God, about the Vicar of Jesus Christ on earth, about the bishop under whose jurisdiction the diocese is placed, then about all Catholics. Now, she wants to name another class of persons, belonging not to the Church Militant, but to the Church Triumphant. She is fully aware that those who are already enjoying the glory of the Church Triumphant are not separated from her, but, on the contrary, that they are intimately united to her, forming but one and the same Church with her. It is true, the Church is divided into the Church Triumphant, the Church Suffering, and the Church Militant; nevertheless there is but one Church. We are to present ourselves, then, before God, in company not only of the saints on earth, but of the saints in Heaven.

For this reason, the priest adds: *Communicantes et memoriam venerantes*.... Yes, we do indeed venerate those whom we are about to name, and our motive for thus honouring their memory is that they have already attained eternal glory and God for evermore; we are united with them, and have direct communication with them, forming but one with them, in the Holy Sacrifice. And who are they?

First of all: *in primis gloriosae semper Virginis Mariae, Genetricis Dei et Domini nostri Jesu Christi*. Our Blessed Lady has every right to an honour peculiar to her alone, and Holy Church never fails to pay it to her; on the present occasion she expresses this her thought by the word *in primis*: it behoves us in the first place, to speak of Mary. Yes, of Mary who always was and ever is a virgin: virgin before birth-giving, virgin in birth-giving, virgin after birth-giving. She is, moreover, the true Mother of God, of Him who is at the same time, our Lord Jesus Christ. All these her titles give her special right to particular mention apart from all others. *Sed et beatorum Apostolorum et Martyrum Tuorum...* Holy Church adds next, the Apostles and martyrs of Christ. She will give us the names of the martyrs presently, but not till she has given us those of the Apostles. Saint Mathias is the only one omitted, but his name occurs later on, in another list, after the Consecration. The name of diptychs is applied to these lists, because they used formerly to be written on folded tablets, frequently of richly carved ivory. Several of these would be used at the altar: on one were inscribed the saints' names to be more particularly commemorated; on another, the name of the reigning pontiff or the patriarch under whose jurisdiction the place was, and of the bishop of that diocese, etc. Sometimes a third was specially added, for the names of the Catholic prince of the country and his children. Finally, those who had founded the Church, in which they were assembled, or who had endowed it, or had rendered it some signal service, had their names also written on a diptych, and as they were particularised, the list was often very long. If any one had the misfortune to fall into heresy, his name would be erased, if inscribed on the diptych, and it could not be replaced there, until he had made due submission and was reconciled to the Church. These customs have now fallen into disuse, because at last the number of persons claiming a right to be inscribed on the diptychs was so great that it became burthensome. The list of saints was then limited and the names fixed as we now have them in the missal; these lists are, however, a remnant of the ancient custom of the diptychs.

Saint Joseph is not mentioned here, no more than he is in the *Confiteor*, because devotion to this great saint was reserved for the latter days, and because just at first, in the earlier ages, the attention of the Church was more specially drawn to the Apostles and martyrs, for all the honours of her worship. Later on, when the time for fixing the Canon came, Holy Church recoiled from rehandling and making modifications, even of smaller details, in a liturgical prayer fixed and consecrated by Christian antiquity. With her ever wise discretion, Holy Church has limited the saints' names mentioned here. Let us go through the list.

Petri et Pauli. The priest has this one thought uppermost in his mind, that he is in close union with all these saints, and that he is engaged in honouring their memory. He names Saint Peter and Saint Paul together, because these two saints are really one, belonging as they both do to the Holy Roman Church which was founded by their joint labours. Then come the other Apostles: *Andreae, Jacobi,* James the Great, *Johannis,* John, the beloved disciple, *Thomae, Jacobi,* James the Less, *Philippi, Bartholomaei, Matthaei, Simonis, et Thaddai,* Thaddeus, called also Jude.

These holy ones just named by the Church, all belong to the Gospel; but in order to show that she belongs to all ages, she deems it well to couple with these venerable names of the very foundations of the Church, others no less dear to her. So these three popes are mentioned in the same list: *Lini, Cleti, Clementis.* Linus, Cletus, Clement, were all three ordained by Saint Peter; so that at the Apostle's death, there were these three bishops in Rome. Saint Peter had appointed Clement to be his successor, but he contrived at first to escape the burthen; nevertheless he was at last forced to accept it, but whether he succeeded Saint Linus, before or after Saint Cletus, on the Chair of Peter, is uncertain. *Xysti,* here we have another Pope; it is Sixtus II, he who had Saint Laurence for his deacon. He is a very celebrated pontiff: he was beheaded in the Cemetery Pretextatus; and the Cemetery of Saint Calixtus where is the Crypt of Saint Camilia, is also called by his name, i.e., of Saint Sixtus. Then follows Cornelius, *Cornelii,* whose epitaph, lately discovered in the catacombs by the Commedatore De Rossi, has been a subject of such lively interest; this epitaph was found in two separate pieces, on one was only *Cor,* on the other, *nelius.*

After these popes, we are given a bishop's name: it is Saint Cyprian, Bishop of Carthage, *Cypriani.* He is coupled, on the diptychs, with his friend, Saint Cornelius. *Laurentii*, the great deacon Saint Laurence ever so markedly honoured by Holy Church. These martyrs all suffered in the persecution under Valerian; but the next, Saint Chrysogonus, *Chrysogoni*, comes under Diocletian. As regards Ss John and Paul, *Johannis et Pauli*, they are much later, being put to death in the reign of Julian the Apostate. Finally, *Cosmae et Damiani*, both physicians; they were not Romans, but their bodies were brought to Rome later; they suffered under Diocletian. These two names close the list adopted by Holy Church, and no others may now be added. She terminates her prayer by naming all the Saints, by whose merits she remends herself to God: *et omnium Sanctorum tuorum, quorum meritis precibusque concedas, ut in omnibus protectionis tuae muniamur auxilio.*

Thus ends this third prayer, which is, like the other two, a prayer of recommendation. First of all, the priest prayed for Holy Church, the pope, the bishop, all Catholics, then for those for whose intention the Holy Sacrifice is being offered; to these he joined other persons in whom he is interested, finally, he reminded God of the union which exists between the Church Militant and the Church Triumphant, and then the names of the saints in Heaven were heard at our altar here below. These three prayers form but one, for which reason, only at the conclusion of this third, the priest, joining his hands, terminates with the usual words: *Per eumdem Christum Dominum nostrum. Amen.* He says the Amen himself and in a whisper; his voice is not to be heard, until the *Pater.*

HANC IGITUR

This prayer being ended, the priest, extending his hands over the oblation, prays anew. This gesture is of high importance and must be here remarked; it comes to us from the Old Law. When a victim was presented in the temple to be offered in sacrifice, the right of the imposition of hands had a twofold meaning and was of double efficacy. The victim was, by means of this rite, set apart for ever from all profane use, and was devoted to the service and honour of God alone. The Lord, thereby, took possession of the victim, whatever it happened to be. So now, Holy Church after having already, at the Offertory, alienated the bread and wine from all profane use, and having offered them unto God, does so now once again, and yet more earnestly, seeing that the moment of Consecration is close at hand. In the holy impatience of an expectation well nigh realised, the priest stretches out his hands over the bread and wine, so that his oblation may have favourable acceptance, before the Throne of God; and he says these words: *Hanc igitur oblationem servitutis nostrae, sed et cunctae familiae tuae, quaesumus Domine, ut placatus accipias: diesque nostros in tua pace disponas, atque ab aeterna damnatione nos eripi, et in electorum tuorum jubeas grege numerari.* Thus, whilst offering the Holy Sacrifice of the Mass, and at this very moment when he is so specially pointing to his oblation itself, the priest prays for himself, for all those who are present, and for all those who are united with them; and he begs that peace may be granted unto us in this world, that we may escape hell, and that we may, together with the elect, enjoy the Glory of Heaven.

There is an addition in this prayer which deserves our notice. Holy Church had not, at first, these words: *diesque nostros in tua pace disponas.* They were added by Pope Saint Gregory the Great, whilst Rome was being besieged by the Lombards, and the city was, consequently, in the utmost peril. Holy Church, since then, has judged it expedient to continue this petition for peace at the present; she was heedful not to retrench from her text words inspired to so holy a pope, by the Holy Ghost Himself, who, as we are told by John the Deacon, often showed Himself visibly in the form of a Dove on the head of Saint Gregory, whispering in his ear what he was to say or do, on certain grave occasions. This prayer ends with: *Per Christum Dominum nostrum,* which words are said by the priest, with hands joined, and to which he adds for himself in a whisper: *Amen.*

QUAM OBLATIONEM

Here begins the great prayer which continues up to the Memento of the Dead, and in the midst of which the sublime Mystery of Transubstantiation is accomplished. Thus speaks the priest: *Quam oblationem tu, Deus, in omnibus, quaesumus, adscriptam, ratam, rationabilem, acceptabilemque facere digneris.* Holy Church continues wholly absorbed in the oblation, imploring of God to bless it, and, in order to this, the priest makes thereon the Sign of the Cross, so that thus sanctified it may be lovingly accepted by the Lord; *adscriptam* (here the Cross is again signed): this oblation is of such real importance, that it must be registered, He is begged to note it down; *ratam* (again, the Sign of the Cross), it must needs be ratified, approved, confirmed in Heaven, as a thing most truly good and fitting; lastly, the priest begs that this oblation may be *rationabilem.* To understand this expression, we must call to mind what those victims of the Old Law were, they were, after all, but gloss and figurative, having no worth, save in as far as they had reference to the Sacrifice of the Cross. Whereas, the bread and wine, or rather—anticipating in thought, together with Mother Church herself, the stupendous effect of the Sacred Consecration, let us say—the Body and Blood of Jesus Christ are here, on our altar, the true and real Victim, the spiritual oblation whereby all other sacrifices are rendered superfluous and sterile, it is in this sense that Saint Paul, writing to the Romans, tells them to offer unto God in their own persons, an interior and wholly spiritual host: *Obsecro vos, fratres per misericordiam Dei, ut exbibeatis corpora vestra hostiam viventem, sanctam, Deo placentem, rationabile obsequium vestrum* (Rom. 12:1). You, who are Christians, says the Apostle, ought to offer your bodies as a living sacrifice, holy, agreeable unto God, and reasonable, that is to say, spiritual, in contradistinction to the Sacrifices of the Old Law. So then, the Christian must offer to God, even his very body, making it to take its share in prayer; and this he does by imposing fasts and penances upon it, in order to prevent its continually dragging downwards, according to its own material tendency; in a word, he must so act that the inferior part be continually upheld, so that it may without hindrance unite itself to the superior part of his being.

But let us return to the offering that is on the altar. Were this bread and wine to remain such as they are they would be no better than the sacrifices of the Old Law; but inasmuch as they are soon to be changed into the Body, Blood, and Soul of our Lord Jesus Christ, verily this will be a *reasonable Host*, essentially *reasonable*. This is not all: our oblation must needs be *acceptabilem*, so that the Lord may truly say: I am wholly satisfied with the offering made to Me. *Ut nobis Corpus et Sanguis fiat dilectissimi Filii tui Domini nostri Jesu Christi.* At the words *Corpus et Sanguis*, the priest makes the Sign of the Cross over the host and over the chalice. Oh! may this oblation become the Body and Blood of Jesus Christ! Truly the Body and Blood of Jesus Christ are for ever in Heaven, but we are asking that They may be produced here below in this oblation which we are offering. So then, it is for our own sakes that we make such a petition to God, as that this oblation may be changed into the Body and Blood of the Lord, for the Church particularly puts these words on our lips: *Fiat nobis*, in order that this Body and Blood may be at our own disposal and may even become our very food.

CONSECRATION OF THE HOST

Quam pridie quam pateretur. These words were added by Pope Alexander I, the sixth successor of Saint Peter. This he did, in order to recall the Passion, because the Sacrifice of the Mass is one and the same with the Sacrifice of the Cross; for the same Lord, when He first immolated Himself in the Cenacle, on the eve of His Sacrifice, was to be immolated the next day on Calvary. *Accepit panem in sanctas ac venerabiles manus suas.* At these words the priest does the very same, he takes the bread into his hands, *et elevatis oculis in coelum*, he too raises his eyes to Heaven, imitating what he is saying that our Lord did. It is not mentioned in the Gospel that Jesus raised His eyes to Heaven, on this occasion, but tradition tells us so—a tradition so certain that Holy Church makes a point of giving it here her full acceptance. *Ad Te Deum Patrem suum omnipotentem, tibi gratias agens.* This is the Eucharist, or thanksgiving; and Holy Church is careful to call attention to it; for, behindhand as we ever necessarily are in paying our ceaseless debt of gratitude to God, for His countless benefits, we should constantly have thanksgiving in our hearts and on our lips. *Benedixit* (at this word the priest signs the Cross upon the host) *fregit deditque discipulis suis. Accipite et manducate ex hoc omnes.* **Hoc est enim Corpus meum.**

The priest then holds the host in both his hands, between the thumb and index finger, and pronounces the words of Consecration, in a whisper, yet distinctly, and keeping his eyes fixed on the host which he intends to consecrate. The moment that these words of Consecration are uttered, the priest, on bended knees, adores the Sacred Host. The rubric says *statim*, at once; he must leave no interval, for the bread has gone, there remain now but the species, the appearances; it has yielded its place to the Lord, it is the Lord Himself whom the priest adores. Rising from his own act of adoration, the priest uplifts the Host, raising It above his head, to show It to the faithful so that they too may adore.

Formerly the Host was not elevated at this part of the Mass, but only just before the commencing of the *Pater.* In the eleventh century, Berengarius, Archdeacon of Angers, having dared to deny the Real Presence of our Lord in the Holy Eucharist, this showing of the Sacred Host to the people, in the Mass, immediately after Consecration was introduced, in order to excite them to adoration.

After this august ceremony, the priest lays the Sacred Host on the corporal and again kneels in adoration before It. From this moment, each time that the priest touches the Host, he will genuflect both before and after doing so; before, because he is going to touch the Lord, and after, in order to pay Him homage. Besides this, he will not disjoin the thumb and index finger of each hand, until the Ablution, because these fingers are sacred, and have alone the honour of touching the Lord. For this reason, at his ordination, the bishop consecrated these fingers in a more special manner, putting the holy oil upon them first, and thence spreading it over the rest of the hand; if a priest were to lose one of his index fingers, he would need permission from the pope himself to touch the Body of the Lord with another finger.

Thus is accomplished the great Mystery of Transubstantiation (that is to say, the changing of one substance into another), according to that word of our Lord to His Apostles: Do this in commemoration of Me: *Hoc facite in meam commemorationem* (Luke 22:19); on condition, however, that the minister be a priest validly ordained, and that he pronounce these sacramental words over true bread and natural wine, with the intention of consecrating as the Church does. These conditions fulfilled, God is not free, He is bound by His own Word, and the Mystery must consequently be achieved.

The word *enim* is put in, to link this phrase with the preceding; it is not to be found in any of the three Gospels which mention the institution of the Eucharist, neither does Saint Paul give it in his Epistle (1 Cor. 11:24). Nevertheless our Lord must have said this word, as this Tradition has come down to us from Saint Peter and the Apostles. A priest who were to omit the *enim* would sin, but his consecration would be valid. If he were to omit the *meam* there would be no consecration, because it is necessary to determine whose Body it is that the priest is holding in his hands.

As soon as these above named sacred words are pronounced, the Body of our Lord is truly on the altar; but because, since His Resurrection, the Body, Blood, Soul, and Divinity of our Redeemer cannot be separated, he is on our altar in a Living State, just as He is in Heaven, that is to say, glorious as He has ever been since His Ascension.

The showing of the Body of our Lord which now takes place, is, as we have explained above, of comparatively modern institution. The Eastern Churches do not observe a similar ceremony, at this part of the Mass; but on the other hand, they give far more pomp and importance, than we do, to the elevation that immediately precedes the *Pater*, and thereby attract the attention of the people to profound adoration: for this purpose, the priest then takes the Body and Blood of the Lord in his hands, and turning towards the faithful, as at the *Orate Fratres*, holds Them up for adoration.

CONSECRATION OF THE WINE

The chalice being uncovered, the priest pronounces these words: *Simili modo post coenatum est* and then taking the chalice into his hands, he continues: *accipiens hunc praeclarum calicem in sanctas et venerabiles manus suas.* Notice this expression, *praeclarum calicem.* How Holy Church extols this chalice which held the Blood of the Lord, and which she is now placing in the hands of her priest! In the Psalm, we have the Prophet telling us: *Et calix meus inebrians quam praeclarus est!* (Ps. 22:5). Yea, truly, my chalice is inebriating! how august is it! how glorious, how magnificent! Mother Church finds this phrase so well suited to the sacred cup which is used to hold the Blood of Jesus Christ, that she now pours out her own sentiments in these very word. The priest continues: *item tibi gratias agens.* The priest spoke previously of this giving of thanks, when, at the consecration of the Host, he said that our Lord, raising His eyes, gave thanks. Then, taking the chalice in his left hand, and blessing it with his right, he says: *benedixit, deditque discipulis suis, dicens: Accipite et bibite ex eo omnes.* The priest thou pronounces the words of Consecration over the wine, whilst he holds the chalice somewhat raised. These are the sacred words: **Hic est enim Calix Sanguinis mei, novi et aeterni testamenti: mysterium fidei: qui pro vobis et pro multis effundetur in remissionem peccatorum.**

Notice that the word *enim* comes in here just as it was at the Consecration of the Bread, to connect what precedes with what is to follow.

The words used for the Consecration of the wine resemble those of the Gospel with some slight differences. We have received them by the tradition of the Church of Rome, founded by Saint Peter, who had himself heard our Lord speak. *Novi et aeterni testamenti.* So then this very chalice of ours holds the Blood of the Lord, the Blood of the New Testament, called also here, eternal, to distinguish it from the Old Covenant which was to last only till the coming of our Lord. *Mysterium fidei*. Mystery, that means the Mystery which specially and above all others, proves our faith; for, according to the word of Saint Peter, our faith must needs be proved. And so truly is It the mystery of faith, that Saint Paul, writing to Timothy, tells him, on the subject of the Eucharist, that deacons should be pure and holy, guarding the Mystery of faith in a clean conscience: *Habentes mysterium fidei in conscientia pura*. It is well known that the Holy Eucharist was given to the special custody of the deacons, who could even administer It to the faithful, in the absence of a priest. Finally, let us notice there other words: *pro multis effundetur in remissionem peccatorum*. This Blood shall be shed for many, unto the remission of sins. Our Faith is that it was shed for all, and not merely for a large number, but all would not profit of It for the remission of their sins.

Such are the words of Consecration of the Wine, the effect of which is so tremendous. They constitute together with the words of Consecration of the Bread, the Sacrificial Act itself. Our Lord is the Victim, the Victim immolated on our altar; not merely in the sense that the Holy Mass, by the mystic separation of the Body and Blood, represents and recalls to us the bloody sacrifice of Calvary; but furthermore, because of the very state and proper destination of the Body and Blood of our Lord, under the Eucharistic Species. Never was victim in any sacrifice, more truly slain and immolated, than is this Divine Victim of ours, as soon as the Consecration is achieved, when He who is the splendour of God the Father, has now no other end and destination for this His Divine Glory, Beauty, and very Life, than to enter into us, there to be wholly lost and consumed.

So then, the Sacrifice is verily and indeed accomplished. God has looked upon It, and we can truly say to Him: behold what was done on Calvary, and were it not for the immortality of Thy Son, the resemblance would be complete. For the accomplishing of this Sacrifice, the priest lends his ministry to our Lord who has bound Himself to come down to be thus immolated each time any mortal man invested with the sacerdotal dignity, holding in his hands bread and wine shall pronounce over them certain words. But who is it that here offers the Sacrifice? Is it the priest, or is it Jesus Christ? It is our Lord Himself, in the person of the priest, who is but one with Him; there is but this single restriction, i.e., that he would not come down on the altar, if the priest did not give his concurrence. The Sacrifice, then, is but one, whether it be offered on Calvary or on the altar.

At the words of Consecration, the priest, while placing the chalice on the corporal, adds the following: *Haec quotiescumque feceritis, in mei memoriam facietis.* When our Lord said this to to his Apostles, He, thereby, gave to them, and in their persons, to all priests, power to do what He had just done, that is to say, to immolate Him. So that, consequently, it is not man who speaks at this solemn moment of the Consecration, it is rather Christ Himself who makes use of man for the purpose.

Such is the dread Christian Sacrifice, which takes us back to Calvary, and shows us how tremendous is the justice of God which required such a Victim. By itself alone, this Sacrifice could have saved millions of worlds. But our Lord willed that it should be perpetuated. Having been immolated once on Calvary, He can do no more; yet, nevertheless, knowing what human weakness is, he feared lest the Sacrifice of the Cross, only once offered, might at last make little impression on the faithful. Before long, man would have treated the Sacrifice of Calvary as a mere historic fact, consigned to the pages of the Church's annals, where few even would think of seeking it. So our Lord said to himself: What was done once on Calvary must needs be renewed until the end of time. See here why, in His Love, he devised this Divine Mystery, whereby He comes into the host and immolates Himself anew. And God too sees the importance of this work, and by its very means He is moved to compassion, and mercy, and pardon towards man.

Now let us next examine and find out who it is that produces this change of the bread and wine into the Body and Blood of our Lord is it that operates in this mystery? It behoves us to remember that whenever any One of the Three Divine Persons of the Blessed

Trinity acts, the other Two Persons concur in this same act, in perfect accord. In the Incarnation, the Son becomes Incarnate but it is the Father who sends Him, and it is the Holy Ghost who operates the Mystery. In like manner, in Holy Mass, the Father sends the Son—the Son comes down, the Holy Ghost operates Transubstantiation, or the changing of the one substance into another. Thus, in order to express the action of the Holy Ghost in this Mystery, the Church in her prayer at the oblation, called upon this Divine Spirit, as we observed, in these words: *Veni Sanctificator Omnipotens, aeterne Deus, et benedic hoc sacrificium tuo sancto nomini praeparatum.*

The Eastern Church has not this prayer, in her liturgy; but wishing, as she does, to make known to the people, the action of the Holy Ghost in this great Mystery, after pronouncing the words of Consecration over the bread, the celebrant says: O Lord, God, deign to send Thy Spirit that He may change this bread into the Body of Thy Son; and all the people answer: Amen. After consecrating the wine, the celebrant again says: O Lord, God, deign to send Thy Spirit that He may change this wine into the Blood of Thy Son; and all the people answer Amen. But this looks like an anomaly; for when the priest utters each of these invocations, Transubstantiation has already been effected. Why then call on the Holy Spirit? This is a remark that has more than once been made; their custom has been maintained, and this is the reason alleged. In order not to mix the acclamation of the people with the words of the Sacred Mysteries, the Eastern Church placed after these the invocations relative to the operation of the Holy Ghost, that is to say, they occur at the very moment chosen in the Latin Church for the elevation, when she presents the Body and Blood of our Lord, to the adoration of the faithful. Then it is that the Eastern Church pays homage to the Power and Work of the Holy Ghost. This, we Latins do, beforehand, both in the prayer: *Veni Sanctificator Omnipotens*, and in the prayer: *Quam oblationem*, in which we say: *Ut Corpus et Sanguis fiat*. Nevertheless, the Latin Church does not ask the people to approve of her prayer by an acclamation; and in this place, would imply the recitation of this prayer, in a loud voice. Now, we have already explained that the prayer of the Canon is entirely secret, and must be wholly recited in a low voice.

UNDE ET MEMORES

The priest having adored the Precious Blood, has shown It to the faithful, and then again adored. He now, once more, extends his hands, and continues his prayer: *Unde et memores, Domine, quaesumus, nos servi tui, sed et plebs tua sancta, ejusdem Christi Filii tui tam beatae Passionis, necnon et ab inferis Resurrectionis sed et in coelis Gloriosae Ascensionis. Offerimus praeclarae majestati tuae....* So do we call to mind. The priest says *we*, for there is question not of himself alone, but of all the people. He reminds God the Father of this; and we all, united with him, call to mind the Blessed Passion, the Resurrection, and the Ascension of our Divine Redeemer. During the oblation, these three great Mysteries were brought prominently forward; but Holy Church is not satisfied with that; she wants to insist on the same thought again, and with still more delight in this place. She well knows that God has done all for man, and she wishes that not one of His Benefits should escape her.

Yea, verily, we are indeed offering a something very great, for we have here before us the Body and Blood of Jesus Christ. We call to mind His Passion which has been so blessed a boon for us; here too the Victim is immolated but more than that, the Victim which we here possess as ours, is also He who rose again. Nor is this even all: we call to mind, likewise, His Glorious Ascension into Heaven. Yes indeed, He who is here present, is the Risen One; He it is, who scaling the Heavens, was seated at the right hand of the Father, whilst the angels re-echoed the glad shout: *Attolite portas, principes, vestras et elevamini portae aeternales, et introibit Rex gloriae* (Ps. 23:7). So then we have really here, upon our altar, Him who suffered, who rose again, and who is now reigning in Triumphant Glory in Heaven. Oh! yes, indeed, we do indeed recall these things, and this it is that gives us such full confidence, that we dare to say with holy boldness:

Offerimus praeclarae majestati tuae de tuis donis ac datis. We talk of offering! We who have nothing! absolutely nothing! Yea, it is true, we have naught of our own, but we offer to Thee Thine own gifts, that is all we can say. This bread and wine were given to us by Thee; then they became the Body and Blood of Thy Son, whom, likewise, Thou didst give unto us, whole and entire; we are then drawing out from Thine own exhaustless riches, and we are offering unto Thee what Thou Thyself hast given us.

And what qualities does this our offering possess? It is pure, holy, and spotless. But, upon earth, all is impure, nothing is holy, everything is tainted and defiled; how then can the priest dare to speak thus? We must recollect what our offering is. It is the very Son of God Himself in whom have been accomplished the great Mysteries of the Passion, the Resurrection, and the Ascension. Behold here what gives Holy Church such boldness of speech. Bride, as she is, she steps forth in face of the Glorious Trinity, and says I am endowed with Thine own riches, I possess him as mine own, who hath performed all this that I am now calling to mind, He is mine, for Thou hast given him to me. Behold now, I offer Him unto Thee, and this my offering is worthy of Thee for It is indeed pure, and holy, and spotless.

This Sacrifice is so powerful, that God is enforced to look upon our offering; He cannot refuse It; and the whole strength of the Sacrifice rests on this, namely, that the Son hath been given unto us, as our own. By Him alone, we realise the four ends of the Christian Sacrifice; we thus lay hold on the part of God Himself, who is obliged to accept this offering, and to own Himself fully satisfied therewith. In the Old Law, it was not so; for how could sacrifices of bullocks and lambs have any such effect upon the great God; what did He want with them? But here, on our altar, under the frail appearances of bread and wine, there is a something which forces the attention of God Himself, and obliges Him to prove unto us that what is offered is indeed acceptable to Him. Well may the devil be enraged at such a sight, well may he make every effort to do away with faith in the Real Presence, striving to overturn our altars, and to diminish the number of priests, so that, at least, fewer Masses be offered unto God. Oh! what a thought is it, that it is a mere sinful man that operates such stupendous things, that stands thus powerful before the very God Almighty! If only this ministry had been reserved unto angels, those pure spirits, untouched by the breath of sin, one could better comprehend it. But no; it is man, sinful man, whom God chooses and whom alone He honours with such a privilege. This man must needs tremble, it is true; but he feels himself all-powerful, holding, as he does, in his very hands, the Son of God Himself.

This host, pure, holy, spotless, which the priest is offering unto God, is moreover: *Panem sanctae vitae aeternae, ac Calicem salutis perpetuae.* Here we have the Eucharist brought before us as the Sacrament. If it is a Sacrifice offered unto God, it is just as truly a Sacrament destined to feed our souls, to give them Eternal Life and Salvation.

In this magnificent prayer, the priest, whilst pronouncing these words: *Hostiam puram, hostiam sanctam, hostiam immaculatam*, makes the Sign of the Cross, thrice, over the Host and the chalice at the same time; then, whilst saying: *panem sanctae vitae aeternae*, he makes it again over the Host; and, when saying: *Calicem salutis perpetuae*, he makes it over the chalice. Can this possibly imply that he here ventures to give his blessing to our Lord? No, assuredly not. Up to the moment of Consecration, he has really blessed the bread, because he has the right to do so, having received sacerdotal powers of giving blessings. But now he holds no longer bread in his hands: it is the Divine Author himself of all benediction who is now upon our altar. If, then, the priest thus makes the Sign of the Cross, it is merely in order to show that this Sacrifice, is the Sacrifice of the Cross Itself, a Sacrifice truly pure, holy, and spotless. He signs the Host separately, in order to express that this is indeed the Lord's very Body, which was crucified; and then the chalice, to signify that it contains the very Blood which was poured out upon the Cross. So we must observe that from the moment of the Consecration, all Signs of the Cross made by the priest are prescribed by Holy Church to indicate and recall the Sacrifice of the Cross; and are in no way meant as signs of benediction made over our Lord.

SUPRA QUAE PROPITIO

The priest again stretching out his hands continues the great prayer, saying: *Supra quae propitio ac sereno vultu respicere digneris.* Yea, Lord, although Thou art infinite Sanctity, infinite Power, Sovereign Being Itself, deign in Thy Goodness and Mercy to cast Thine eyes upon this earthly dwelling of ours, and vouchsafe to incline Thy Face unto that which we are now offering unto Thee: *supra quae respicere digneris.*

Et accepta habere. Formerly, up to the time of Saint Leo, this prayer did not end in the way it now does; the word *illa*, those things, was understood here, as the complement of the phrase. Saint Leo thought it would be better to give it a more determined close, and so he added these words to the said prayer: *Sanctum sacrificium, immaculatam hostiam.* Such then is the real sense: *et accepta habere sanctum Sacrificium, immaculatam hostiam.* The remainder of the phrase forms a kind of parenthesis to the preceding, as it now stands: *sicuti accepta habere dignatus es munera pueri tui justi Abel.* Receive, then, O Lord, this Sacrifice (says the priest), as Thou didst accept the offerings of Thy servant, the just Abel. The gifts of Abel, O Lord, were agreeable unto Thee; and yet what he offered was infinitely inferior to that which we are now able to present unto Thee: there is no comparison possible, between these two Sacrifices; nevertheless, lowly as was Abel's sacrifice, Thou didst graciously accept it.

Nor is this all; there was yet another ancient sacrifice that God held dear: *et sacrificium patriarchae nostri Abrahae*, it was the sacrifice of Abraham. The first-named, that of Abel, was in a bloody manner, but Abraham's was unbloody: it was a father's sacrifice, consenting as he did, to the immolation of his son, demanded by God. The Lord said unto him: Take thy son and go and offer him to Me in holocaust, on the mountain that I will show thee. And Abraham obeyed God, and set out with his son. The whole consisted in this acquiescence of the great patriarch; his sacrifice was all spiritual, for God, contented with his obedience, bade him spare his son; the blood shed on this occasion was but that of a ram, immolated instead of Isaac. Abel and Abraham are coupled in this Sacrifice of Jesus Christ, who has given up His honour and His Life, offering unto His Father devoted-ness the most complete, immolating himself truly, since His Body and Blood are here separated before Him. It is then most fitting to recall here the sacrifice of Abel and that of Abraham; observe also how the sacrifice of blood is primordial, but still that of Abraham is so agreeable unto God, that, in return, it makes this holy patriarch become the direct ancestor of Christ, who truly had flowing in his veins the blood of this father of the faithful.

Further still, the priest here adds other words whereby is proved the existence of a third sacrifice: *et quod tibi obtulit summus sacerdos tuus Melchisedech*. This third sacrifice is wrapped in mystery: it was offered by the high priest Melchisedech, himself a mysterious personage, and God found his offering truly acceptable. We can here remind Him of what He Himself says to His Divine Son, in Psalm 109: *Tu es Sacerdos in aeternum secundum ordinem Melchisedech.* Yes, O Lord, when Thou wishest to honour Thy Son, Thou dost tell Him He is priest according to the Order of Melchisedech; how agreeable, then, unto Thee must not the sacrifice of this mysterious person have been. In the Holy Mass we have at once united, the sacrifice of Abel, that of Abraham, and that of Melchisedech: the sacrifice of Abel, which represents the Sacrifice of the Cross, with which the Mass forms but one and the same Sacrifice; the sacrifice of Abraham, in which the immolation takes place in an unbloody manner, as is the case in the Sacrifice of the Mass; finally, the offering of Melchisedech which represents the Sacrifice of the Mass, in which bread and wine are used upon the altar; but, after Consecration, there remains neither bread nor wine, but only the species or appearances, serving but to veil the Divine Victim.

SUPPLICES TE ROGAMUS

During the following prayer, the priest no longer has his hands outstretched, because he is bowing down, in lowly supplication; placing his joined hands on the altar, he says: *Supplices Te rogamus,*

Omnipotens Deus: jube haec perferri per manus sancti Angeli tui in sublime altare tuum, in conspectu divinae Majestatis tuae. Dread words are these, says Innocent III, in his treatise on the Mass! The priest designates his offering by the simple word *haec, these Things;* he knows that God sees them, and knows their priceless worth, so he contents himself with merely saying: *jube haec perferri,* command that these things be carried.

And whither does he want them to be carried? *in sublime altare tuum.* This altar of ours here on earth suffices us not; we aspire even so far, as that this our offering may be placed on that altar which Saint John saw in Heaven, and on which he pictures to us a lamb, as it were, slain: *et vidi Agnum stantem tamquam occisum.* This lamb is standing, says Saint John; nevertheless, he adds: *tamquam occisum,* as it were, slain. Truly, our Lord will ever bear the marks of His Five Wounds, but, now all resplendent as suns; and this Lamb is standing, because He is living, and dieth now no more; thus does Saint John show Him unto us. Such is the altar, on which the Lord standeth, in His Immortal Life, bearing the marks of what He has suffered for us: *Agnum tamquam occisum,* there is He for ever, before the Throne of Divine Majesty. So now, the priest begs of God to send His angel to take up the Victim from this our altar on earth, and to place It on the altar of Heaven.

To what angel does the priest here refer? There is neither cherub, nor seraph, nor angel, nor archangel that can possibly execute what the priest here asks God to command to be done. It is an act wholly beyond the power of any created being. Now, observe the meaning of the word angel; it signifies *sent,* and the Son of God was the *One Sent,* by the Father; He came down upon earth among men, He is the true *Missus,* sent, as He says of Himself: *Et qui misit me Pater* (John 5:37). Our Lord is not simply in the rank of those spirits whom we term angels and archangels, placed near to us by God. No, He is the angel by excellence, He is, as the Scripture expresses it, the angel of the Great Counsel, *Angelus magni consilii,* of that great Counsel of God whereby willing to redeem the world, He gave His own Son. So then, the priest begs of God that the angel may bear away *haec* (*What is upon the altar*), and may place It upon the altar of Heaven; he makes this petition in order to show the identity of the Sacrifice of Heaven, with the Sacrifice of earth.

Here we have something similar in idea, to what is found in the Greek liturgy. After the Consecration, the Orientals beg of the Holy Spirit to come down and operate the Mystery, as we before noticed, in order to show that it is the Holy Ghost who works here, just as he operated in the Blessed Virgin. The act is accomplished, it is true, and the Greek priest should refrain from such a prayer, seeing that, without it, the Holy Ghost has already operated the Mystery. But no; this is but their way of affirming what we have just seen expressed in the Latin prayer we are now studying, namely, the identity of the Sacrifice of the Lamb, whether on the altar of Heaven or that of earth. In Heaven, the Lamb is standing, although, as it were, slain; here below, He is in like manner slain. Now who is it that can make these two Sacrifices, to be both one? It is Jesus Christ, the sent, the angel of the Great Counsel.

The priest then adds: *ut quotquot ex hac altaris participatione.* The priest kisses the altar, whilst pronouncing these words. Holy Church has the profoundest veneration for this altar which represents Jesus Christ, who is himself the living altar; therefore, in its sanctification and consecration, does she lavish her most beauteous rites. The priest continues: *Sacrosanctum Filii tui Corpus et Sanguinem sumpserimus* (here he signs with the cross the Host and chalice, as also himself), *omni benedictione coelesti et gratia repleamur. Per eumdem Christum Dominum nostrum.* So we here beg to be filled with all graces and blessings, just as if we were already admitted in Heaven, to the participation of that living altar there, Jesus Christ, who sheds around Him grace and benediction. We crave these graces and blessings, in virtue of our participating at this altar of earth, which Holy Church treats with such veneration. It is in the name of this altar that the priest asks all sorts of blessings for all mankind. Observe how the priest never speaks for himself alone, so here he says *repleamur*, that we may be filled, he signs himself with the cross, whilst saying these last words, in order to show that this benediction comes to us by the Cross, and also to signify that we accept it with our whole heart. Here ends the second part of the Canon, that which is consecrated to the offering. These three prayers wrap the Act of Consecration, just as the preceding ones prepared for it. Now, Holy Church would bring us back to Intercession.

MEMENTO OF THE DEAD

Besides the Church Triumphant and the Church Militant, there exists a third part of this Great Body. Yes, God has given us the power to intercede for the Church Suffering, to come to her aid and to do her good; therefore the Holy Sacrifice can be offered in behalf of her suffering members, and Holy Church in her maternal love, wishes that in every Mass that is said, mention should be made of them, because thereby fresh succour is procured for those of her children who are still detained in this place of expiation. It is a point of Faith that the Holy Sacrifice brings relief to the souls in Purgatory. This doctrine has been handed down to us by Tradition. As early as the second century, we find Tertullian speaking of prayer for the dead. There used, formerly, to be a separate diptych set aside exclusively for the names of the departed, whose memory was particularly to be preserved—benefactors, for example.

The priest now addresses himself to God, in behalf of these suffering members: *Memento etiam, Domine, famulorum famularumque tuarum N. et N. qui nos praecesserunt cum signo fidei et dormiunt in somno pacis.* We say that we are interceding for those who have gone before us, with the sign of faith. What does the Church understand by this sign of faith? It is the sign of Baptism, and that of Confirmation, which latter makes the perfect Christian. Baptism alone already gives us the sign of faith, because in it we are marked with the Cross, so truly so that when the body of a deceased person is brought to the Church, the priest pronounces this prayer over it: *Non intres in judicium cum servo tuo, Domine...qui, dum viveret, insignitus est signaculo sanctae Trinitatis.* Yes, it was signed with the sign of faith, *signum fidei,* the sign of the Trinity; it is therefore entitled, O Lord, to be taken into consideration by Thee, and not to be judged too severely. This expression of Holy Church, *signum fidei*, gives a proof, once more, that we may not here pray for infidels, as we have already noticed above, speaking of the *Memento* of the living, since they are not in communion with Holy Church.

Et dormiunt in somno pacis. Holy Church puts here strongly before us, in what light she regards death in the case of a Christian. It is a sleep, she tells us, for those of whom we speak, *dormiunt*; for the same reason she gives the name of cemetery to places reserved for burial, because this word means a dormitory, or sleeping place. Yes, they sleep and it is the sleep of peace, *in somno pacis*. Holy Church uses this expression, because those for whom she is praying, died in peace with her, and in true filial submission to her; they died in Jesus Christ, in the kiss of the Lord; even were they still in Purgatory, it can yet be said of them, that they sleep in peace, because they are saved in Jesus Christ, who bringeth peace along with Him. In the catacombs these words *in pace* are frequently found graven on tombstones; this was the early Christians' way of speaking of death; so too, in the Office of Martyrs we sing: *Corpora sanctorum in pace sepulta sunt*. This very ancient Office recalls the language of the catacombs: *in pace*. Holy Church preserves a vestige of the same, when praying for her dead, she bids the priest say: *dormiunt in somno pacis*.

The rubric here directs the priest to join his hands when ending this first part of the prayer. Then it is that he prays for such of the deceased as he more particularly wishes to recommend. Having done so, again stretching out his hands, he continues thus *Ipsis, Domine, et omnibus in Christo quiescentibus*; here we see that every Mass is of profit to all the souls in Purgatory. *Locum refrigerii, lucis et pacis, ut indulgeas, deprecamur.* Notice here these three things asked for by Holy Church refreshment, light, and peace. Now, what is Purgatory? It is a place in which souls stand in need of refreshment, for those piercing flames are keenly felt. Moreover, it is a place where there is no light, since Holy Church craves for these poor souls, *locum lucis*; so there is nothing ever in this place of expiation, to distract them from their fearful sufferings. Furthermore, it is a place where sweet peace reigns not; there, is ceaseless agitation, the soul striving towards God whom it may not reach; there, in direst trouble and anguish, the misery of the poor soul in having thus put herself into such straits of wailing sorrow and frightful pain. Yes, Purgatory is indeed a place the very opposite of that abode where reign endless *refrigerium, lux, et pax.* These three expressions are of the highest importance, because they reveal to us, that whenever we pray for the dead, the succour that reaches them by our means, is always in the form of refreshment, light, and peace.

The priest terminates the prayer, in the usual manner: *Per eumdem Christum Dominum nostrum. Amen.* Besides this, there is a special rubric which bids him bow his head whilst saying these concluding words, which is not prescribed in the case of closing other prayers. It is meant as one more earnest pleading; for at this moment, light shines in Purgatory, as prayer offered for these poor souls can never be ineffectual. As it were, the dismal prison is uncovered now, to allow the sweet dew of refreshment, light and peace to distil gently on those burning sufferers; and this triple aid is given to the different souls, in the proportion assigned to each by the justice of God; for Holy Church can only pray for the dead, by way of suffrage; she has no longer those rights she had over them when they were her members on earth. But, on the other hand, we also know that her prayer has always a salutary effect on the souls suffer in Purgatory, and that God never allows any prayer said in their behalf to be of no avail.

NOBIS QUOQUE PECCATORIBUS

Now having shown how the Precious Blood of Christ has flowed plentifully in Purgatory, let us turn our thoughts upon our selves. The priest is going to speak in his own and our interest. He declares himself a sinner, as we ourselves are. *Nobis quoque peccatoribus famulis tuis, de multitudine miserationum tuarum sperantibus partem aliquam et societatem donare digneris cum tuis sanctis.* We also, although sinners, claim our share of happiness; we would not be excluded from it. This is the only occasion on which the priest speaks aloud during the Canon; and whilst thus speaking, he strikes his breast, and the faithful should do in like manner. Our fraternal charity has urged us to pray for such of our brethren as are dead, and have not, as yet, been admitted into a participation of the bliss of Heaven. But, we beseech our Lord, that He would give us to partake of the like happiness; it is in his goodness and mercy, that we put our trust.

And with whom is it that we desire to have a share and fellowship? *Cum tuis sanctis Apostolis et Martyribus:* with thy Holy Apostles and martyrs. It seems to Holy Church, that she has not as yet named a sufficient number of saints; but still not deeming it fitting to add other names to her first list, she found this moment a favourable one, for speaking of those that had rendered themselves especially dear to her. As it is a most marked glory for the saints that their names should thus be registered in what is the great act of the Church—therefore has God chosen His elect that are thus to be commemorated in the very presence of Jesus Christ Himself. Here, again, we meet afresh with Apostles and martyrs: *Cum tuis sanctis Apostolis et Martyribus.* Neither must we forget, that, in the early ages, the *Cultus* of mere confessors was not, as yet, established; holy honours were only given to Apostles and martyrs: it is for this reason that these are the only two classes mentioned. Therefore we desire to be with them; and then also *cum Johanne*: with John. Who is the John that is mentioned here? It is John the Baptist, our Lord's Precursor. *Stephano*, with Stephen, the Protomartyr. Why has not this model, this first of martyrs, been named until now? Because, in the first diptych, after having mentioned Saint Peter and the Apostles, Holy Church passed on at once to the first Popes: Linus, Cletus, and Clement. By thus naming Saint Peter and his three successors, the Church is straightway established, as is the power of Peter, by this glorious trinity of holy popes. Saint Stephen's name would have deranged this order of ideas, had he taken his place in the first list. The same

87

must be said of Saint John the Baptist, who is looked upon neither as an Apostle nor a martyr, although he preached penance and the coming of Christ, and although he was put to death because of the earnestness wherewith he took up the cause of Chastity: the Church, however, desirous of mentioning these two great saints, assigned them this place. *Matthia*, with Mathias: here we have an Apostle. The reason of his name being put here, is, because, as Holy Church enumerated twelve Apostles on her first diptych, adding Saint Paul to the twelve—Mathias, who was chosen to complete the Apostolic College, after Judas's apostasy, was not to forfeit the right to his position, and it was but fair to put his name at the head of the second diptych. *Barnaba*, with Barnabas, the companion of Saint Paul in many of his evangelical travels. *Ignatio*, with Ignatius, the great martyr, who after Evodius, had succeeded Peter in the See of Antioch. He it is, who wrote that magnificent Letter to the Romans, wherein he speaks of the happiness that awaits a Christian, when he may have the happiness of dying for Christ. He came to Rome under Trajan, as it were, to mingle his ashes with those of Peter and Paul; for it was in that city that he suffered martyrdom. *Alexandro*, with Alexander: here comes the name of a great pope. He was the fifth or sixth successor of Saint Peter. It was a happy thought to insert his name here; for, it was he that prescribed that these few words should be put in the Canon: *Qui pridie quam pateretur*, (who the day before he suffered,) and this in order to recall to our minds, at this solemn moment, the memory of the Passion. *Marcellino, Petro*, with Marcellinus and with Peter. These are two of those who suffered in the persecution of Diocletian. Marcellinus was priest, and Peter exorcist. Their names are never separated. So far there has been no mention made of any holy woman, in the Canon. Holy Church could never omit them. Who, then, is the first she speaks of? *Felicitate*—with that great Felicitas, the mother of the seven martyred children, who thus renewed under the persecution of Marcus Aurelius, the generous sacrifice of the mother of the Maccabees. So illustrious was she, together with her children, that the catacombs being already opened at the period of their martyrdom, the Christians divided amongst them the bodies of her children, in order to place them in the various cemeteries. Felicitas was martyred on the 29th of November; whereas her children had been thus honoured in the preceding July. She was buried in the cemetery of Priscilla, together with two of her sons. *Perpetua*, this is that noble lady of Carthage. As her name is put after that of Saint Felicitas, this affords us an additional proof that this Felicitas is certainly the one of Rome, and not she who suffered at Carthage together with Perpetua. In this place Perpetua represents her companion as well as the rest who suffered with her; she is emphasised as being the foremost among them all, and as having written certain portions descriptive of her martyrdom. *Agatha, Lucia*, with Agatha, Lucy: Until the time of Saint Gregory the Great, they used to say: Perpetua, Agnes, Cecilia but this holy pontiff, loving Sicily, where he had himself founded six monasteries, inserted in the Canon the names of the two Sicilian virgins, Agatha of Catania, and Lucy of Syracuse. Out of courtesy, due to strangers, he gave them the precedence of the two Roman virgins, Agnes and Caecilia. Why then does Agnes come in here before Caecilia? She did not suffer until under Diocletian, whereas Caecilia is to he found under Marcus Aurelius. Perhaps, harmony of phrase is the sole real reason for this. *Anastasia*, she is the noble Roman widow who suffered martyrdom under Diocletian, and who is so illustrious at Rome, that formerly the sovereign pontiff used to celebrate the second Mass of Christmas Day in her Church. Although this practice is now discontinued, a commemoration of this great saint is still made in that same Mass—*Intra quorum nos consortium, non aestimator meriti, sed veniae quaesumus, largitor admitte.* After having mentioned the saints anew, the priest begs that God would deign to admit us amongst them; not assuredly because of any merit of ours giving us any right thereunto, but because God's goodness, mercy, and pardon are able to do so (but of thine own gratuitous pardon). The priest terminates by the ordinary conclusion: *Per Christum Dominum nostrum.*

PER QUEM HAEC OMNIA

In former times a certain ceremony was here observed, which is now discontinued. There were brought and placed near the altar, bread, wine, vegetables, and fruits, whilst the priest pronounced the following words (which are still said immediately after the conclusion of the preceding prayer): *Per quem omnia, Domine, semper bona creas, sanctificas, vivificas, benedicis et praestas nobis.* Whilst, saying these words, the priest, who is then standing in the very presence of our Lord himself, and in all the grandeur of his sublime ministry, gave the blessing to everything at that moment presented at the altar. The difference which is to be found between the customs observed in former times and those of our own day, at once explains both the existence of this ceremony in the early ages and its omission in later centuries. Formerly, each Church had only one altar, which was placed and arranged according to what is described by Saint John in the Apocalypse. In the furthest recess of the mysterious apsis was the throne of the Father, in front of which was the altar, the ancients on each side thereof, and the lamb placed thereupon. One only Mass was said and this even not always every day; it was celebrated by the bishop, all the priests joining with him and consecrating together with him. The faithful then would come presenting the fruits of the earth and whatever serves as food, to be blessed by the bishop at this single Mass. Later on, about the eighth century, there was developed, by the secret impulse of the Holy Spirit, a popular devotion for the more frequent celebration of Holy Mass. Altars were multiplied, and the number of Masses increased. But in proportion as this custom was introduced, that of bringing fruits and vegetables to be blessed was gradually discontinued.

What, then, would Holy Church do with these words of benediction? The priest turns them, now from their primitive sense, and applies them to the Body of our Lord Jesus Christ, present on the altar, by *whom* all things are given unto us. Thus, even the priest signs with the cross the chalice and Host at these words *Sanctificas, vivificas, benedicis.* Perhaps this appears somewhat strained; but at any rate it shows us how great is the respect of Holy Church for the sublime prayer of the Canon. In order not to lose these few words, she prefers now to apply them to the Body of Jesus Christ, which was created, which by the Mysteries of His Passion, of His Resurrection, and of his Ascension, accomplishes what is expressed by these words: *vivificas, benedicis, et praestas nobis*, for It is given to us as Food.

We have just a vestige left of this ancient ceremony, in these our days. On the feast of the Transfiguration, grapes are blessed at this same moment; but the words used for this purpose are not those of the Canon. The prayer made use of by the Benedictines is taken from the Cluny-Missal. In the same way also, on Maundy Thursday, it is at this same moment that the bishop blesses the oil of the sick.

The Canon is nearing its close; it will terminate with the priest raising his voice to say its concluding words, and to recite the Lord's prayer. The Greeks call the Canon *the Liturgy*. In the course of ages the signification of this word was extended so as to express the whole aggregate of that which composes the entire Divine Office; but originally it was strictly understood of the Canon of the Mass only, which is *the work* by excellence, as the Greek word expresses it. In the same way, we find marked, in the Latin missal: *infra actionem*, to signify that which is done in the action of the Sacrifice; that is to say *the Action* by excellence. Furthermore, the very word *Canon* is also a Greek word, as we have before remarked; and there is nothing surprising in this, since it is well known how widely spread was the use of the Greek tongue, at the period of the birth of Holy Church. Out of the four Gospels, three were certainly written in Greek.

Before the conclusion of the great prayer, a very solemn rite is performed; it is Holy Church's last confession of the identity existing between the Sacrifice of the Cross and that of the Mass. The priest uncovers the chalice containing the Blood of our Lord, and after making a genuflection, he takes in his right hand the Sacred Host, and in his left hand the chalice, then he three times makes the Sign of the Cross with the host, over the chalice, going from one lip of the chalice to the other, saying: *per ipsum, et cum ipso, et in ipso*—then, making the Sign of the Cross between the chalice and his own breast, with the sacred Host, as before, he adds: *est tibi Deo Patri omnpotenti, in unitate Spiritus Sancti*: he replaces the Host above the Chalice and slightly elevates both saying: *omnis honor et gloria*, he then puts down the Host again, and recovers the chalice; and having done so, says: *Per omnia saecula saeculorum*, and the people answer: *Amen*.

What does this action of the priest signify? Holy Church possesses her Spouse in the state of immolation and of sacrifice; nevertheless, He is living. Thence she would here bring out, in a marked manner, this His character of the living God, and she expresses it by thus reuniting the Body and Blood of the Lord, placing the Host immediately over the Precious Blood, in order to give Glory to God. She then bids the priest say: *per ipsum*, by Him is the Father Glorified; *et cum ipso*, with Him is He glorified, because God the Father has not a glory superior to that of the Son, nor isolated from that of the Son (see what majesty in this *cum ipso*); and, *in ipso*, in Him is the Father glorified: the glory, which is brought by the Son to the Father, is in the Son, and not outside of Him, *in ipso*. Thus, by Him, with him (that is to say, conjointly with Him), and in Him, are all honour and glory to God the Father. The priest, twice again, makes the Sign of the Cross, but this time he makes it between the chalice and his own breast. And why this difference? He is pronouncing these words: *est tibi Deo Patri omnipotenti, in unitate Spritus Sancti*; as neither the Father, nor the Holy Ghost have been immolated, it would be unbecoming, whilst naming them, to place the Host over the Blood which belongs to the Son alone, Who alone was clad in our human nature, and alone was immolated for us. But whilst pronouncing these last words: *omnis honor et gloria*, the priest again holds the Sacred Host over the chalice, expressing thereby, that in the veins of the Divine Victim that he is offering, the Precious Blood flows together with immortality for evermore. So the priest can now say to God: *omnis honor et gloria*; this offering is the most glorious act that can possibly be made to thine honour, for we possess the risen Christ, and it is His very self that is immolated to Thine honour, on this altar. No, He who is offered is not a mere creature; but by

Him, and with Him, *per ipsum et cum ipso*, are all honour and glory to God. Thus, this glory goes straight to God; He cannot refuse the homage which is paid to Him, which is rendered by Him who is immolated, but yet is living still. The Sacrifice thus truly offered indeed, is the greatest act which can be done for God. On Calvary, the immolation of our Lord was a hideous and abominable crime; but here, this immolation is all that is most glorious for God, and it is so, because He who is offered is living. It is the Living God we offer; it is the Living Son offered to the Living God. What more grand, what more just, than to express this thought by placing the Body of our Lord directly over His Blood? See here how it is that the Sacrifice of the Mass is the most glorious Act that can he done for God, since all honour and all glory are rendered to Him at this sublime moment; *per ipsum, et cum ipso, et in ipso.*

This solemn rite, of which we are treating, shows us how much God has loved the world. When we consider that He whom the priest is thus holding in his hands, is not only He by whom all glory is given to God, but even He who shares this same glory together with Him: *per ipsum, et in ipso!* It is the Word of the Father who allows himself to be lifted in one's hands, to be touched, because He wishes that all glory should be given to God, *omnis honor et gloria*, He wishes that there should ascend to God a homage from which He cannot turn away. What now are all the homages of men compared with the worship paid by our Lord Himself to His Father!

Yes, the Holy Sacrifice of the Mass is verily the most glorious act we can possibly do for God; one can offer a prayer, or perform an act of virtue, but that does not force the attention of God; whereas at the Mass He is forced, by all this own infinite perfections, to be attentive to the worship there paid Him.

Now let us see if this important rite can be traced up to the first centuries. It is certainly very ancient; it must have existed in all ages, as it is to be found everywhere. It can at once be understood that Holy Church, offering up her Spouse unto God, could never say that He is dead; she has immolated Him, it is true, but He whom she has thus immolated is living and this she must needs confess.

Lo! now are accomplished the three great Mysteries, the Passion, the Resurrection, and the Ascension. That our Christ is indeed our very own, is what these three Mysteries truly express, and Holy Church right well remembers it. Before these were accomplished, there was not so much richness, if we may be allowed the expression. He was born at Bethlehem, but the Incarnation alone was not to save us, according to the designs of God; although it would have sufficed thereunto and superabundantly, if such had been the Divine Decree. Then, Christ suffered His bitter Passion, but that was not enough; there must be his victory over death, His Resurrection. There must yet be something more. Christ must open Heaven, He must have His Ascension; it needs must be, I say, that our human nature, which He deigned to take to Himself, in which He suffered, by means of which He subjected Himself to death—that this very human nature should be throned in Heaven—His Ascension, therefore, is a very necessity. So truly and indeed, He whom we hold in our hands, is the Lord himself, He who suffered, He who died, He who hath risen again, He who hath ascended into Heaven.

Behold here the reason why we owe great thanks to our Lord, for having allowed us to be born since the accomplishment of all these stupendous Mysteries. For in the case of those who died between the taking place of the Resurrection and the Ascension, although happier far than those who preceded them in point of time, still are we much more fortunate than they, for in their day, Christ was not as yet completed in his Mysteries. Those who died between the death of our Lord and His Resurrection, were less happy than the first named; and as to those who died before our Saviour, they had but the hope, and they were obliged to quit this life, before seeing this hope realised. Oh! how far more highly favoured are we, than those who have gone before us! and so we say: *unde et memores Domine, nos, servi tui, sed et plebs tua sancta ejusdem Christi Filii tui Domini nostri tam beatae Passionis, nec non et ab inferis Resurrectionis, sed et in coelos gloriosae Ascensionis.* What energy in these words! But moreover what profound reverence, and what love ought we not to have for one single Mass, since it is the one grandest thing which our Lord

Himself has done! It is even all that He can do; it is that which He will ever do, for the ministry of our Lord is never to cease; priest He is and ever will be: *tu es sacerdos in aeternum.*

It is His Father Himself who declares the perpetuity of His priesthood: *Juravit Dominus et non paenitebit eum: tu es Sacerdos in aeternum secundum Ordinem Melchisedech.* The Lord hath sworn it, *juravit:* thou art priest for ever, saith He, according to the order of Melchisedech. The Lord adds this, because Jesus Christ is to exercise His ministry by means of bread and wine which were likewise the matter of the sacrifice of Melchisedech. Priest, then, is He for ever, offering Himself ever for us, living for ever; and all this, as Saint Paul says in order to make intercession for us: *Semper vivens ad interpellandum pro nobis;* yet retaining ever the wounds of His Passion, so as to bespeak the sacrifice and to offer these His wounds to His Father for us. Confidently then, does Holy Church say to God: *Jube haec perferri per manus Sancti Angeli tui in sublime altare tuum, in conspectu divinae Majestatis tuae,* that is to say, these things which we are here offering, in order that they may be wholly one with that altar yonder in Heaven, since of this they are truly worthy. For on the altar of earth, just as on the altar of Heaven, it is always and ever Jesus Christ who is the offerer, being priest for ever, and who is likewise, at the same time, the Victim also. Yea even when the world ceases to exist, our Lord will continue to render unto God, the very same worship, in his quality of priest: *Sacerdos in aeternum,* because it is meet that God should be honoured for ever. Nevertheless, the two ends of Sacrifice which regard propitiation and impetration shall exist no more; Jesus Christ, *Sacerdos in aeternum,* will continue only to adore and give thanks.

It is well to remark here, that the Sacrifice of praise surrounds the Sacrifice of the Mass, whereby true life is given to the former. Holy Church has fixed the hour of Tierce for the offering of the Holy Sacrifice of the Mass. This was the hour at which the Holy Ghost came down upon the Church; hence at the beginning of this hour we are bid, in the Office, to say: *Nunc Sancte nobis Spiritus.* The Church invokes this Divine Spirit who by His very presence gives warmth to her love and prepares her to offer the Great Sacrifice. Ever since Matins, the entire Office has been lighted up by the beaming rays of this sublime Sacrifice; and this its influence will last on, even unto the Compline hour, which concludes the Sacrifice of Praise.

Formerly, as we have already said, the Elevation used to take place at the end of the Canon. The Greeks have retained this Custom which is observed as follows. The priest having placed the Host above the chalice and said the words: *Omnis honor et gloria*, turns towards the assembled faithful, holding the Body and Blood of our Lord, which he shows to the people, whilst the deacon utters aloud these words: *Sancta Sanctis*, holy things for the holy!

The great prayer of the Canon being terminated, the priest interrupts the silence which reigns in the holy assembly, by exclaiming: *Per omnia saecula saeculorum.* And the people answer: *Amen*, as a sign of approbation of what has just been done, and of union with the offering just presented to God.

THE LORD'S PRAYER

Our Lord has told us: "When you would pray say: our Father who art in Heaven, hallowed be Thy name…." What better occasion could there be than the present, of making this prayer to God? So the priest now, is going to let us hear the *Pater noster.* As in our own day, so in all past ages, the Lord's prayer has had a place in the course of the Holy Sacrifice, for we meet with it in every liturgy and in every Canon of the Mass. Moreover, it is used by the Church, on all solemn occasions; it is our support; it is the pledge which our Lord has given us, saying: when you would pray, say: *Pater noster.* Holy Church preludes this prayer, with these magnificent words: *Praeceptis salutaribus moniti, et divina institutione formati, audemus dicere.* Yes, if we dare to speak, if we formulate the petitions which follow, it is because we rely on the very precept which we have received so to pray, a precept given us by our great Master for our salvation. Thus have we been instructed by His own Divine Mouth, so we dare to say, *audemus dicere: Pater noster.*

The priest is about to present to God successively, the seven petitions of the Lord's prayer. The first three regard God Himself and treat, therefore, of the love of benevolence, thus does our Lord set us on the road of the purest love. *Pater noster qui es in coelis, sanctificetur nomen tuum*, hallowed be thy name, that is to say, let all honour and respect be paid to it as it deserves, because that is thy very right. *Adveniat regnum tuum.* Thy kingdom come that is, we beg that thy reign be established in all and over all, because thou art truly king. *Fiat voluntas tua sicut in coelo et in terra.* Thy Will be done on earth; that is to say, by men, as it is in Heaven, by the angels and the blessed.

Having thus prayed, following the teaching of our Lord Himself, that God's kingdom may come, that His Glory may be realised in all creation, the priest adds the other four petitions of the Lord's prayer, which treat of that which is necessary for ourselves. *Panem nostrum quotidianum da nobis hodie.* Here we ask for our daily bread; God so understands it, and our Lord thus points out to us, by bidding us say only daily bread, that it is useless to be preoccupied without cause, seeing that we do not even know if we shall be alive tomorrow. But we are asking bread, not for the body only, but also for the soul, which likewise needs food. For this reason, one of the Evangelists has it: *panem nostrum supersubstantialem da nobis hodie* (Matt. 6: 11). Lo! this bread is on the altar; there it is to feed our souls; and now is the moment to ask It of God. Then, as we are sinners, it behoves us to beg for pardon. *Et dimitte nobis debita nostra, sicut et nos dimittimus debitoribus nostris*; yea, forgive what ever we have done against thee. And we ourselves mark the measure of this our pardon, by begging Him to forgive us, as we forgive them that trespass against us. This does not mean that man's forgiveness is the measure of God's, but that the more mercy we show to others, the more will be extended to ourselves. *Et ne nos inducas in tentationem*, and lead us not into temptation, that is to say, ward and defend us when temptation strikes us. Although it be in the designs of God that we should thus be tried, in order that we may gain merit, still may we beseech Him to spare us therein, for we are weak and may so easily fall.

Sed libera nos a malo, but deliver us from evil. Here two things must be understood: we ask to be delivered from evil, from the evil one, that is the devil, who is ever seeking to make us fall into evil. Moreover, if we have committed it, we beg of God mercifully to withdraw us from its grasp.

LIBERA NOS QUAESUMUS

Here begins another part of the Mass, which continues up to the second prayer before the Communion. Communion is the means taken by our Lord to unite all men one with the other, so as to make of them all, one whole. Thus when Holy Church would drive forth from her bosom one of her members who has rendered himself unworthy of her, she excommunicates him; he has no longer any share in this communion of the faithful. In order to express this union, Holy Church wishes that peace, the result of that charity which reigns amongst the faithful, should be the object of very special attention. So now, she is about to ask it, in the following prayer; and then presently, the kiss of peace will be mutually given amongst the faithful and will give expression to their charity one with the other.

Our Lord hath said: if whilst offering thy gift at the altar, thou rememberest that thy brother hath something against thee, leave there thy gift before the altar, and go first and be reconciled with thy brother; and then coming, thou mayest offer thy gift. Holy Church entering fully into this thought of her Lord, is here occupied at this solemn moment, with the maintenance of peace and charity amongst all her members. In Masses of the Dead, this kiss of peace is not given, thus keeping ever in view, that the dead being no longer under power of the keys of Holy Church, she cannot give them peace; our relations with them are utterly changed.

The priest, therefore, says, as if developing the last petition of the Lord's prayer: *Libera nos, quaesumus, Domine, ab omnibus malis praeteritis, praesentibus et futuris*. Yea, Lord, strengthen us, because our past evils have caused us to contract spiritual weakness, and we are as yet but convalescents. Deliver us from the temptations of which we are now being made the butt, and from the other afflictions which are weighing us down, as well as from the sins of which we may be guilty. In fine, preserve us from those evils which may be lurking for us in the future. *Et intercedente beata et gloriosa semper Virgine Dei Genitrice Maria, cum beatis Apostolis tuis Petro et Paulo, atque Andreae et omnibus sanctis.* Holy Church, standing in need of intercessors, fails not to have recourse to the Blessed Virgin, as well as to the Holy Apostles Peter and Paul. But why is Saint Andrew alone, here added on to these? Simply because the Holy Roman Church has ever had a very special devotion to this Apostle. *Da propitius pacem in diebus nostris, ut ope misericordiae tuae adjuti, et a peccato simus semper liberi, et ab omni perturbatione securi.* Give us, Lord, peace in these our days, so that aided by the help of Thy mercy, we may be delivered, in the first place, from all sin, and then be secured against all evil attacks that might surprise us unawares.

Such is this magnificent prayer of Peace, which is used by Holy Church for this special Mystery of Holy Mass. Towards the middle of this prayer, just when the priest is saying *et omnibus Sanctis*, he makes the Sign of the Cross with the paten, which he has been holding in his right hand, from the commencement; he then kisses it, as a mark of honour to the sacred vessel on which the Body of the Lord is about to repose: for it is never permitted to kiss the host Itself. The prayer being ended, the priest places the paten under the host, he uncovers the chalice, takes up the host and holding it over the chalice, breaks it through the middle, whilst saying this portion of the concluding words: *Per eumdem Dominum nostrum Jesum Christum Filium tuum.* He then replaces, on the paten, the part of the host which is in his right hand, and breaks off a particle of the other half which he is holding in his left hand, saying: *qui tecum vivit et regnat in unitate Spiritus Sancti Deus;* then placing also on the paten the portion of the host which he has in his left, and holding over the chalice the small particle which he has just broken off, he says in a loud voice: *Per omnia saecula saeculorum.* The people, in approval of his petition and making it also with him, answer: Amen. Then making three times the Sign of the Cross over the chalice, with the particle, he says aloud: *Pax ✠ Domini sit ✠ semper vobis✠cum. ℞. Et cum spiritu tuo.* Holy Church never loses sight of the peace for which she has just been asking, and she here profits of this moment to refer to it again.

The priest then allows the particle which he had in his hand, to fall into the chalice, thus mingling the Body and the Blood of the Lord, and saying at the same time: *Haec commixtio et consecratio corporis et Sanguinis Domini nostri Jesu Christi, fiat accipientibus nobis in vitam aeternam. Amen.* What is the meaning of this rite? What is signified by this mingling of the particle with the Blood which is in the chalice? This rite is not one of the most ancient, although it is quite a thousand years old. Its object is to show, that, at the moment of our Lord's Resurrection, His Blood was reunited to His Body, by flowing again in His veins as before. It would not have sufficed if this soul alone had been reunited to His Body; His Blood must necessarily be so likewise, in order that the Lord might be whole and complete. Our Saviour, therefore, when rising, took back his Blood which was erstwhile spilled on Calvary, in the Praetorium, and in the Garden of Olives.

We may here mention a custom of the Orientals which has only been introduced since their separation from the Church, and certainly a very whimsical and venturesome usage, dating only from the fourteenth century. After the Consecration, a chafing dish is placed on the altar, upon which boiling water is kept hot, from this at several intervals small quantities are taken and mingled with the Precious Blood, but so, however, as not to alter the Sacred Species.

In the prayer which the priest recites whilst mingling the particle of the host with the Precious Blood, the word *consecratio* must not be taken in the sense of sacramental consecration, but simply as signifying the reuniting of Sacred Things.

AGNUS DEI

After this mingling, the priest bowing before the Most Holy Sacrament, and joining his hands, recalls the words of Saint John Baptist and says: *Agnus Dei, qui tollis peccata mundi, miserere nobis.* These words could hardly be better introduced than now. Thus it is that Holy Church is wont to seek everywhere, the most lovely things in order to blend them together in one beautiful whole, in the great action of the Holy Sacrifice. Therefore does she take up the song which the angels sing in Heaven, and she too cries with them: *Sanctus, Sanctus, Sanctus, Dominus Deus Sabaoth.* Then she adds the gladsome shout of the Hebrew children: *Benedictus qui venit in nomine Domini.* But now she sings with the precursor *Agnus Dei.* Yea, at this moment, the Lord is verily and indeed Himself the immolated Lamb, and twice does she implore of him, who hath taken our sins upon him, to have mercy on us, *miserere nobis.* The third time she adds: *Dona nobis pacem,* because the Eucharist is, as we have said, the Sacrament of peace, by means of which all the faithful become united together.

In Masses of the Dead, instead of *miserere nobis,* there is said *dona eis requiem,* and the third time, *sempiternam* is added, which very clearly expresses the character of the petition we are making for the souls of the faithful departed; we are asking for them, not now, as formerly, union in peace, but rest in the Eternal Peace.

PRAYERS BEFORE THE COMMUNION

Now comes the prayer of peace: *Domine Jesu Christe, qui dixisti Apostolis tuis, pacem relinquo vobis, pacem meam do vobis, ne respicias peccata mea, sed fidem Ecclesiae tuae, eamque secundum voluntatem tuam sanctificare et coadunare digneris. Qui vivis et regnas Deus, per omnia saecula saeculorum. Amen.*

Such is the formula whereby the priest petitions for peace and union amongst the faithful, at the very moment when they are about to partake of the Holy Mysteries. This prayer is not said in Masses of the Dead. When it is ended, the priest who is celebrating the Mass, gives the peace to the deacon, who gives it to the subdeacon, by whom it is passed, in like manner to the choir. If the celebrant is a bishop, he gives the peace to the assistant priest, who, in his turn, passes it to the choir, whilst the deacon and subdeacon approach to receive it directly from the prelate himself.

As to the celebrant, he takes the peace, by kissing the altar, in front of the Sacred Host. Thus, it is our Lord Himself who gives it to him. A plate of precious metal (called for that reason *instrumentum pacis*), may be used for the giving of the peace; in which case, the celebrant kisses this plate, after having kissed the altar. Should there be present any princes, princesses, or other personages of high rank whom it is fitting thus to honour, the *instrumentum pacis* is taken to them, to kiss in their turn.

We have already remarked that the peace is not given in Masses of the Dead; the same omission is observed on Maundy Thursday, as a protest against the kiss of Judas, whereby he betrayed our Saviour, delivering him up into the hands of His enemies. On Holy Saturday, likewise, the *kiss of peace* is not given, thus keeping up the ancient custom peculiar to that day, when its celebrations took place during the night hours; and this because the great number of neophytes might have then occasioned confusion. Another reason, too, for its omission on Holy Saturday, is that it was not until the evening of Easter Day, that our Risen Lord addressed the disciples assembled together, with the words: *Pax vobis*. Out of respect for the least details in the life of her Divine Spouse, the Church omits, for one and the same reason, in the Mass of Holy Saturday, both the *Agnus Dei*, wherein occur the words: *dona nobis pacem*, and the ceremony of the *kiss of peace*, for the resuming of which she waits until the Mass of Easter Day.

The priest has yet two other prayers to recite before the Communion. Those now found in the missal are not very ancient; nevertheless, they are at least a thousand years old. Formerly, what was said at this moment was traditionary, just as were the prayers of the Offertory; so that these prayers are not to be found in the Sacramentary of Saint Gregory, which contains only the Prefaces, the Canon, and the Collects, Secrets, and Postcommunions. All the rest was transmitted by Tradition, and varied in the several Churches. The two now fixed in this missal were chosen from out of the variety of prayers thus handed down. These two prayers are always said, even when the prayer of peace is omitted.

The first of these begins thus: *Domine Jesu Christe, Fili Dei vivi, qui ex voluntate Patris, cooperante Spiritu Sancto, per mortem tuam mundum vivificasti.* Lo! in the death of our Lord, the whole Blessed Trinity acts; the Father wills it, the Holy Ghost co-operates and assists the sacred humanity of our Lord in the voluntary offering that He makes of Himself. But let us continue the prayer: *libera me per hoc Sacrosanctum Corpus et sanguinem tuum, ab omnibus iniquitatibus meis, et universis malis.* The first thing we ought to desire, when approaching Holy Communion, is that our sins may disappear; and as we have not the present moment alone in view, we moreover beg to be freed from all evils, adding this petition regarding the future: *et fac me tuis semper inhaerere mandatis et a Te numquam separari permittas. Qui cum eodem Deo Patre et Spiritu Sancto vivis et regnas Deus in saecula saeculorum. Amen.* Here three things are begged by us, of the God who is coming unto us in the Holy Communion: first, that we may he delivered from our sins; then, that we may ever adhere closely to his commandments; and finally, that He would never allow us to be separated from Him.

Let us now pass on to the third prayer: *Perceptio Corporis tui, Domine Jesu Christe, quod ego indignus sumere praesumo, non mihi proveniat in judicium et condemnationem.* This is in allusion to the words of Saint Paul about the Holy Communion, when he says, in his first Epistle to the Corinthians: *qui enim manducat et bibit indigne, judicium sibi manducat et bibit* (1 Cor. 11:29). The prayer terminates with these words: *sed pro tuae pietate prosit mihi ad tutamentum mentis et corporis, et ad medelam percipiendam. Qui vivis et regnas.* There is here an evident oversight on the part of the liturgists who composed this prayer. In all the others, care has been taken to mention both the Body and the Blood of our Lord, whereas, in this place, the Body alone is named. This prayer might almost appear little needed, were it not for its striking use in the Good Friday's Function. On that day, the priest really does receive under the species of bread alone, but he is not then offering the Holy Sacrifice. For the immolation of the

Victim, the two species of both bread and wine would be necessary, But on Good Friday, the memory of the Great Sacrifice effected on Calvary, so completely occupies the thought of Holy Church that she recoils from renewing it on the altar. She confines herself merely to partaking of the sacred mystery, by Communion; and in so doing, she makes use of this third prayer, to the exclusion of the preceding, in which mention is made of the Sacrifice. This prayer can very appropriately be used by the faithful when about to communicate.

These prayers being ended, the priest says the following words, which are a free rendering of Psalm 115: *Panem coelestem accipiam, et nomen Domini, invocabo.* Holy Church never loses an opportunity of drawing from the Psalms; because she there finds the true source, model, and type of prayer.

Having pronounced these words, the priest takes up in his left hand, the two portions of the host, beneath which he holds the paten; and, striking his breast three times, he says: *Domine, non sum dignus ut intres sub tectum meum; sed tantum dic verbo, et sanabitur anima mea.* These were the words addressed by the centurion to our Lord, who was coming to heal his servant. Once again let us repeat, Holy Church is ever showing how she possesses the happy secret of choosing the loveliest passages of Sacred Scripture, to place in the Holy Mass; as it were enchasing them there, like priceless diamonds! We likewise say *Domine non sum dignus*.... In our case, it is not for our servant that we beg a cure; it is our own poor soul craving help for herself, and making use of these words as a last appeal to God. We sorely need to be cured; and the nearer we approach the Lord who alone can cure us, the greater should be our confidence in asking. Assuredly nothing can be so certain and manifest, as our unworthiness; but, on the other hand, who is so powerful as the Lord. There is nothing for us, but to appeal to Him, and crave with true humility: *sed tantum dic verbo, et sanabitur anima mea.* Yea, say but one word, and my soul shall be healed!

COMMUNION

After this act of humility the priest disposes himself to make his Communion; signing himself, therefore, in the form of a Cross with the host, which he holds in his right hand, he says: *Corpus Domini nostri Jesu Christi custodiat animam meam in vitam aeternam. Amen.* Let us observe the words, *in vitam aeternam*, unto Life Eternal. The priest speaks as if he were to communicate but once only in his life. One communion would of itself be sufficient to preserve our soul unto Life Eternal, for such is the intrinsic efficacy of this Divine Sacrament, provided for our wants by God. Of this truth our Lord has vouchsafed to give occasional examples, amongst others, that of Saint Mary of Egypt, who being bidden to prepare herself for Holy Communion, received It from the hand of the holy Abbot Zozimus; and this one only Communion did verily preserve her soul unto Life Eternal. Observe also, that this Divine Sacrament is not a pledge of Life Eternal for the soul alone, it is likewise a pledge of the body's future resurrection. Thus, when the bishop gives Communion to newly ordained priests, he says to each one, *Corpus Domini nostri Jesu Christi custodiat te in vitam aeternam.*

Having communicated, the priest pauses a moment in recollection, and then uncovering the chalice, he puts therein the small particles of the host, which may have adhered to the corporal and paten; whilst doing so he says these words: *Quid retribuam Domino pro omnibus quae retribuit mihi? Calicem salutaris accipiam, et nomen Domini invocabo.* What return shall I make to the Lord, for all He hath rendered to me? I will take the Chalice of Salvation and will call on the name of the Lord. These words are culled from Psalm 115; in speaking here of the chalice, *Calicem Salutaris*, David had no common kind of drink in view; the prophetic phrase here stands out clearly; one already catches a glimpse of man to be saved by a potion with which none other may compare, a potion which is no other than the very Blood of his Saviour. Then the priest adds: *Laudans invocabo Dominum, et ab inimicis meis salvus ero.* Now, will I praise the Lord, for my tongue is now fitted for his praise, by reason of the gifts He has given me; and being delivered from mine enemies, I shall have nothing more to fear, He then takes the chalice in his right hand and making the Sign of the Cross with the chalice itself, says: *Sanguis Domini nostri Jesu Christi custodiat animam meam in vitam aeternam. Amen.* Then he receives the Precious Blood as well as the particle which he mingled therewith at the moment when he was addressing his wish of peace to the people.

This is now the proper time for communicating the faithful, if any approach to receive; if not, the priest at once purifies the chalice. The server pours a little wine into the chalice which is presented to him by the priest, who says: *Quod ore sumpsimus, Domine, pura mente capiamus. Et de munere temporali fiat nobis remedium sempiternum.* These words are very ancient, as may be seen by noticing the Latin itself, which is very fine, quite classic, in fact. Remark the expression, *munere temporali*, this is said because Communion belongs to time. God is Eternal, it is true, and he gives himself in Communion; but nevertheless, this Communion itself takes place on a certain day, and at a determined hour and moment: hence it is truly a temporal gift. But by means of this very gift, our Lord achieves the union of the soul with himself; and as he is Strength Itself, he turns this singular act of His into a remedy, the energising faculty of which, should last for ever, and thus is the soul cured.

Then, a second time, the priest has wine put into the chalice, by the server; but on this occasion, water is mingled with it; he purifies his fingers at this moment, and thenceforth he can disjoin them. Whilst these things are being done, the priest says: *Corpus tuum Domine, quod sumpsi, et sanguis quem potavi adhereat visceribus meis, et praesta: ut in me non remaneat scelerum macula, quem pura et sancta refecerunt sacramenta, Qui vivis et regnas in saecula saeculorum. Amen.* This prayer, like the preceding, is also very fine and is certainly very ancient: both of them, in fact, as well as the prayer of peace, must be dated from the first ages. At the first Ablution the priest puts wine only, into the chalice, out of respect for the Precious Blood, with which the chalice is still moistened, and of which something may yet remain. For this reason, it is prescribed that, in case an accident should occur and this wine be spilled, it must be treated with the same respect as the Precious Blood itself, and whatever it has touched must be purified. Rubricians recommend the priest to turn this wine all round the inside of the chalice, so as to gather up with it, every smallest drop of the Precious Blood that might possibly be still remaining therein.

At the second Ablution, water is mingled with the wine, because the Blood of our Lord is no longer there. The priest must always drink from the same side of the chalice; and for this reason, a small cross is always engraven on its foot. Without this precaution, the priest would be liable, if he were not very attentive, to wipe off, with the purificatory, the Precious Blood still wet on the lip of the chalice.

POSTCOMMUNION

All these things being completed, the priest, after saying *Dominus vobiscum*, recites the final prayer, which is now called the Postcommunion, but which, in the Sacramentary of Saint Gregory was designated as: *Oratio ad complendum*. No mention is there made of the Communion antiphon being to be said by the priest, because this being one of the sung parts, has no place in the Sacramentary. It was but the antiphon of a Psalm, sung during the Communion. We have a vestige of this custom in the Mass of the Dead. It was the same also with the Introit, the chanting of which used to accompany the priest from the moment of his quitting the sacrarium till he reached the altar.

This prayer called the Postcommunion is an important one: in it, mention is always made of the Communion just received. It is immediately followed by the ordinary good wish of the priest to the people: *Dominus Vobiscum*. Then the deacon, turning towards the assembly of the faithful, intones the following words:

ITE MISSA EST

These words are usually translated thus: "Go, the Mass is said." However, we must here observe that this is not their proper sense. This
formula, adopted by the Church, was in general use amongst the
Romans, in public assemblies, to announce the termination of the
meeting. So, these words: *Ite, concio missa* est, meant "go, the assembly
is dismissed." In the early ages, the Holy Sacrifice was never called
by our word *Missa*, the Mass. When the Sacrifice was finished, the
assembled faithful were dismissed by the deacon, in the form usual
at all public meetings. Later, the word *missa* having been adopted,
the confusion of ideas became complete, when by the putting of a
capital M to this formula, it ended in *Ite Missa est*, being thus translated amiss: Go, the Mass is said. In Masses at penitential times, in
Lent, for example, instead of the *Ite Missa est*, the deacon says *Benedi-
camus Domino*; the faithful are not dismissed, because it is supposed
that they would like to remain longer in prayer, during these days
of expiation. The *Ite Missa est* is consequently a sign of joy, and, as
such, it is excluded from Requiem Masses: a song of joy would be
out of keeping with a Mass breathing only sadness and supplication.

The *Ite Missa est* having been said, the priest turns again to the
altar, and bowing somewhat, with his hands joined, he says: *Placeat
tibi Sancta Trinitas obsequium servtutis meae, et praesta ut Sacrificium,
quod oculis tuae majestatis indignus obtuli, tibi sit acceptabile, mihique et
omnibus, pro quibus illud obtuli, sit, te miserante, propitiabile. Per Christum
Dominum nostrum. Amen.* This prayer is a kind of epitome made by
the priest, reminding the Holy Trinity of all he has just been doing,
begging acceptance of this Sacrifice, and that it may be profitable
to all those for whom he has been praying.

THE BLESSING

After this prayer, the priest kisses the altar, raises his eyes to Heaven,
stretches out his hands, and then bows before the Cross, saying:

Benedicat vos omnipotens Deus, then turning round to the people, he adds, blessing them: *Pater, et Filius, et Spiritus Sanctus*; to which they answer: *Amen*. A simple priest should only give the blessing once, even in solemn Masses; whereas, bishops, by way of distinction, give it thrice. Prelates likewise bless three times, when they celebrate pontifically. Some of them are even allowed to do so in a Low Mass; but if so, it is only by privilege. The blessing is not given in a Requiem Mass, because it is a sign of joy which would ill contrast with the mournfulness pervading the function.

THE LAST GOSPEL

The blessing having been given, the priest goes to the Gospel side of the altar, and there reads the beginning of the Gospel according to Saint John. Formerly, the priest having no book in front of him, used to make the Sign of the Cross on the altar before signing himself. The cards on which are written the prayers of the Ordinary of the Mass, with the exception of the Canon, and which we nevertheless call altar-canons, are of very recent date. Since their introduction, it has become customary to make thereon, at this moment, the Sign of the Cross; but the priest is still allowed to make it on the altar, which is the figure of Christ who died upon the Cross for us, whose twofold generation this Gospel recounts.

But why is this reading made? The custom originates from the Middle Ages. At that period, as in earlier times also, the faithful had a great devotion to the having a portion of the Gospel read over them, and the commencement of that of Saint John was a special favourite. Demands at last became so multiplied, that the number of priests was insufficient to satisfy all: to simplify the matter, it was decided to recite it over all those assembled, at the end of the Mass. The devotion of the faithful, therefore, alone originated this addition. When a saint's feast is kept on Sunday, or on some feria having a proper Gospel, the priest substitutes this Gospel for that of Saint John. This too is but a consequence of the custom introduced of reading the Gospel at the end of the Mass, and it dates only from the time of Saint Pius V. The pontifical itself has not accepted this change on the ancient usage and hence a pontiff recites the Gospel of Saint John, whilst coming down from the altar.

Let us here remark that in this phrase of Saint John's Gospel: *Omnia per ipsum facta sunt*, the Latin Church, up to the time of Saint Pius V, followed a mode of punctuation different from that used by the Greeks. Saint Augustine and all the Latin Fathers, as well as Saint Thomas read it thus *Sine ipso factum est nihil. Quod factum est, in ipso vita erat, et vita erat lux hominum*; whereas Saint John Chrysostom, and, in general, the Greek Fathers read it: *sine ipso factum est nihil quod factum est. In ipso vita erat, et vita erat lux hominum*. Manuscripts having neither full stops, nor commas, (the use of which was only introduced much later,) this diversity was produced; and Saint Pius V, in his edition of the Missal, kept to the Latin punctuation, for this passage. But shortly after him, the custom of reading it according to the manner of the Greeks, was introduced into the West.

When the priest comes to these words of the Gospel of Saint John: *Et verbum caro factum est*, he genuflects in honour of the annihilation of the Word made flesh, who emptied Himself, taking the form of a servant (Phil. 2:7).

The Gospel being ended, the priest comes down from the altar, after bowing to the Cross; and as he retires, he recites the canticle *Benedicite*, together with the other prayers of thanksgiving marked in the missal.